AYN RAND is the author of *Atlas Shrugged*, philosophically the most challenging bestseller of its time. Her first novel, *We the Living*, was published in 1936, followed by *Anthem*. With the publication of *The Fountainhead*, she achieved a spectacular and enduring success. Rand's unique philosophy, Objectivism, has gained a worldwide audience. The fundamentals of her philosophy are set forth in such books as *Introduction to Objectivist Epistemology*, *The Virtue of Selfishness*, *Capitalism: The Unknown Ideal*, and *The Romantic Manifesto*. *Journals of Ayn Rand*, *The Ayn Rand Reader*, and *The Art of Fiction* are available in Plume editions. Ayn Rand died in 1982.

ROBERT MAYHEW, Ph.D. is an associate professor of Philosophy at Seton Hall University. He is the editor of *Ayn Rand's Marginalia* and has lectured extensively on Rand.

PETER SCHWARTZ is chairman of the board of directors of the Ayn Rand Institute, as well as an instructor of an advanced writing course at the Institute's Objectivist Graduate Center.

AYN RAND

The Art of Nonfiction
A Guide for Writers and Readers

EDITED BY ROBERT MAYHEW
INTRODUCTION BY PETER SCHWARTZ

A PLUME BOOK

PLUME
Published by the Penguin Group
Penguin Putnam Inc., 375 Hudson Street, New York, New York 10014, U.S.A.
Penguin Books Ltd, 27 Wrights Lane, London W8 5TZ, England
Penguin Books Australia Ltd, Ringwood, Victoria, Australia
Penguin Books Canada Ltd, 10 Alcorn Avenue, Toronto, Ontario, Canada M4V 3B2
Penguin Books (N.Z.) Ltd, 182–190 Wairau Road, Auckland 10, New Zealand

Penguin Books Ltd, Registered Offices: Harmondsworth, Middlesex, England

First published by Plume, a member of Penguin Putnam Inc.

First Printing, February 2001
10 9 8 7 6

"The Politics of Fear and Hope" by James Reston from *The New York Times*, May 6, 1969.
Copyright © The New York Times Company, 1969. Reprinted by permission.

(P) REGISTERED TRADEMARK—MARCA REGISTRADA

LIBRARY OF CONGRESS CATALOGING-IN-PUBLICATION DATA:
Rand, Ayn.
    The art of nonfiction: a guide for writers and readers / Ayn Rand ; edited by Robert
    Mayhew ; introduction by Peter Schwartz.
        p. cm.
    Includes index.
    ISBN 0-452-28231-4
    1. Authorship. I. Mayhew, Robert. II. Title.

PN147 .R35 2001
808'.02—dc21
                                                                                    00-045666

Printed in the United States of America
Set in Goudy
Designed by Eve L. Kirch

CONTENTS

CONTENTS

INTRODUCTION

To all the practitioners—and to all the discouraged, might-have-been practitioners—of the art of nonfiction writing, the author of this book offers an invaluable service: she de-mysticizes writing.

The process of writing is widely regarded as an impenetrable mystery. Good writing, it is believed, is the product of some inborn ability, which can be neither objectively defined nor systematically learned. Like ardent religionists who insist that the road to truth is open only to those who are visited by divine revelation, many teachers of writing claim that the path to effective prose can be traversed only if one is struck by the inexplicable thunderbolt of inspiration.

Ayn Rand rejects this idea. She maintains that writing is a rational sphere, governed by rationally identifiable principles.

"Writing is no more difficult a skill than any other, such as engineering," she says. "Like every human activity, it requires practice and knowledge. But there is nothing mystical to it." Since writing is essentially the act of communicating your thoughts clearly, it can be done competently by virtually everyone: "Any person who can speak English grammatically can learn to write nonfiction. . . . What you need for nonfiction writing is what you need for life in general: an orderly method of thinking."

In analyzing the process of writing, her starting point—unlike that of other theorists—is not the content of the writer's mind, but the source of such content: the facts of reality. On this philosophic issue, Ayn Rand was an unyielding advocate of the Aristotelian view, which she described as the primacy of existence—the view that the universe exists independent of anyone's awareness of it, that the function of consciousness is to grasp, not to create, reality, and that the absolutism of existence is what ought to shape one's thoughts (and actions).

This is the premise that underlies her approach to writing. Repudiating the standard, subjectivist perspective, she holds that writing is to be treated as an objective science: "Whenever you have a problem, whether you are writing an article or building a doghouse, do not look *inside* for the solution. Do not ask: 'How do *I* do it? Why don't *I* know it?' Look *outside* and ask: 'What is the nature of the thing I want to do?'" From this, she proceeds to discuss the nature of writing and its consequent requirements, such as the strict need to delimit one's subject and theme, or the indispensability of an outline. She provides clear, perceptive principles about the psychological process of writing (such as the different roles played by the conscious mind and the subconscious), along with methodical advice to guide you through the process (from getting ideas, to choosing your subject and theme, to polishing your draft).

The primacy of extrospection over introspection leads to another important principle of writing. Ayn Rand urges writers to direct their attention solely to their work—to what is needed to do it well, to how to solve problems that arise—but not to its supposed meaning for one's worth as a person: "If you have difficulty with writing, do not conclude that there is something wrong with you. Writing should never be a test of self-esteem."

Of course, according to the mystical viewpoint, the writer's self-esteem will always be at issue. If writing is a matter of being zapped with inspiration by a gracious muse, the absence of such inspiration must indicate unworthiness on the writer's part.

One of the worst consequences of that viewpoint is the mental torture it inflicts upon writers. If the content of your consciousness arises causelessly, independent of reality, then writing is a journey not into the unknown, but into the unknowable. If there are no firm rules by which to proceed—if one must stare passively at an empty page or empty screen, with mind idling, waiting desperately for the muse to hit the accelerator—then writing must be laden with anxiety and guilt. It is tantamount to trying to design a computer with no principles of electronics or mechanics, only the hope of somehow being moved by the right "spirit."

Since writing should be regarded as a science, Ayn Rand says, the job of the writer is at root no different from that of the scientist. "It would never occur to a scientist to focus partly on his experiment and partly on his self-esteem or future fame. (If it does, he is a neurotic and will probably not be heard from.) He has to focus exclusively on his experiment. Nothing else is relevant. The same applies to writing, only it is harder because it is a purely mental job—there is nothing in reality yet except a blank sheet of paper. This is why so many people fail at it. It is harder to focus on the reality of what you have to produce when there is nothing before you but a blank page. . . . In practice, you must be *more* reality-oriented than a scientist, who has the help of the physical problem and the physical objects he is working with."

This is not just the de-mysticizing, but the de-agonizing of writing. Ayn Rand's methodology will not make writing problem-free, but something much better: problem-solvable. The conviction that one's work can be guided by rational principles rescues writers from a sense of helplessness. It saves them from the state of pre-science savages, who felt they were at the mercy of incomprehensible forces. Such a feeling is paralyzing to a writer, who has to know that, *in principle*, he is in control of his work—that his success depends, not on some inscrutable emanations from his gut, but on identifiable ideas from his brain.

Those who are serious about writing should find this approach enormously rewarding. I know that after reading an early transcript of this material years ago, I found the process of writing much easier and more enjoyable. The approach presented in this book makes writing a definable—and thus readily doable—activity, rather than a debilitating battle. I use much of this material in a writing class I teach at the Objectivist Graduate Center of the Ayn Rand Institute.

And the response I typically get from students is something along the lines of: "So there *is* a definite method by which to write—and it works!"

The transcript I originally saw was merely a verbatim account of Ayn Rand's extemporaneous remarks. In this book, by contrast, her presentation has been impressively reorganized, with material taken painstakingly from one corner of the transcript and moved to another, where it logically belongs. Robert Mayhew deserves abundant praise for his editing, which has resulted in a much more integrated and readable product.

Those who experience the process of writing as overwhelming and traumatic will, I expect, find this book liberating. During the Renaissance, scientists—armed with the revived Aristotelian confidence in the power of reason—came to realize that the world was theirs to conquer. Writers, armed with Ayn Rand's de-mysticizing approach to writing, can be similarly unleashed, with the world of words theirs to master.

—Peter Schwartz
Danbury, Connecticut
July 1999

EDITOR'S PREFACE

In 1969, Ayn Rand gave a course on nonfiction writing to well over a dozen friends and associates. At the time, she was editor of *The Objectivist* magazine (Objectivism is the philosophy she originated); she gave the course to help those who were, or planned to be, contributors.

She did not deliver prepared lectures. Instead, she spoke on a topic (some evenings for over three hours) guided solely by a brief outline. These "lectures" were interspersed with: general discussion; requests for clarification, with her replies; discussion of homework assignments; and question-and-answer periods.

The course was privately recorded. My task was to convert the recording into a book. Let me describe the kinds of editing I did.

Cutting. A great deal of material had to be cut, though I am confident that nothing of importance pertaining to nonfiction writing was omitted. (Prompted by student questions, Ayn Rand occasionally went off on fascinating tangents into philosophy, politics, and art. Much of what she said is of great interest, and such material will no doubt be published in some form eventually; but it does not belong in this book.) In regard to nonfiction writing, I assumed that every passage of hers was worthy of inclusion unless I could make a case for its omission. If, for example, while she was lecturing, a student interjected a question, and her brief reply added nothing to the discussion (because it was repetitive or dealt with a narrow problem of no general interest), I omitted it. Or if the students spent two hours discussing their outlines or writing samples with her, I did not include the entire discussion. However, I always tried to incorporate into the book any important insights or principles that she mentioned during these discussions.

Reorganizing. Ayn Rand did not present this course as a series of lectures corresponding exactly to the chapters of this book. How, then, was her course organized?

When it began, she did not have a complete picture of what material would be covered, or even how many times the class would meet. Nor did she have in mind an exact order of presentation. On the first night, she told the class:

> As late as this afternoon, I wasn't yet sure whether I would be giving a *series* of classes. Originally, I thought we might cover everything in one evening. Well, that's where I'm not omniscient: Since then, I made a brief outline of the main topics that I know of (which does not yet include any questions you may have). If we finish everything in ten lectures, we will be doing very well.

In fact, it took them sixteen evenings, meeting usually every other week, to "finish everything."

Whatever was undecided at the outset, the basic logical structure of the core of the course was clear to Ayn Rand from the start. This core is found in chapters 1–8; this is where she covers the central aspects of nonfiction writing. Here she had a definite structure in mind, and I followed it. No major reorganization was required.

The material in the remaining chapters (9–12) is not part of what she considered the "main topics" of the course. These chapters instead consist of her extensive answers to questions on miscellaneous topics in regard to nonfiction writing—all too good to omit. With one exception, Ayn Rand answered these questions in the order in which they were asked, and so I had to determine the proper order of presentation in a book. I did place "Acquiring Ideas for Writing" (chapter 12) last because she indicated that this issue could best be covered at the end. Since there was no formal conclusion, I ended with the story she herself used to end the course.

Given the extemporaneous nature of her presentation, and the extent of student participation, there were numerous digressions— for example, she would often return to points discussed earlier, or respond to questions or comments on later or tangential issues. Part of my job was to integrate this material into a logical presentation. Thus, within every chapter it was necessary to some extent to shift material around.

Line editing. My aim here was to ensure that the writing was clear and readable. This involved transforming Ayn Rand's oral presentation into written form, i.e., condensing what she said, eliminating repetitions, and, where necessary, correcting grammar.

Notwithstanding the amount of editing required, it is remarkable how lucid her extemporaneous material is. But there are occasions when the recording is unclear or contains gaps. In most of these cases, no educated guess at a meaning was possible, and so the passage was omitted. In rare cases, it was almost, but not absolutely, certain what her meaning was; here the wording necessary to make the passage fully clear was supplied.

Because of the number of editorial changes I made, it would have distracted the reader had I used the apparatus of brackets and ellipses. Therefore, I use brackets only for text that could not have come from Ayn Rand. For example, if she referred to something she had said three months earlier, I would change it to, say, "as I discussed in [chapter 1]."

My purpose was not to turn Ayn Rand's remarks into a smooth, finished piece of writing. Rather, it was merely to help in making the course clearer and more readable. I believe I have fulfilled this task, and I am pleased with the results. But this book, I stress, still retains the quality of an extemporaneous presentation. Ayn Rand never intended her unprepared remarks in 1969 to be transformed into a book. In fact, in answer to a student's question about the nature of a first draft, she said: "When I give these lectures, I speak from an out-line, and my subconscious fills in the concretes. If you transcribed a recording of them, that would be like a very rough first draft. But it would *not* be good enough to publish." In my judgment, however, it is eminently "good enough" now to read.

If you wish to see or judge the merits of Ayn Rand's own writing, please consult the works that she *did* intend for publication.

I wish to thank, most of all, Leonard Peikoff for allowing me to undertake this project, for his superb and extensive editorial guidance during its first stages, and for giving the entire manuscript a final editing. The principles of editing he taught me will continue to be useful well beyond my work on this book. Many thanks to Peter Schwartz as well, for writing the introduction, and for his excellent editorial advice in the last stages of the project. His work on this book has improved every page. I also want to thank the Ayn Rand Institute for its help, which took many forms. Finally, and as always, I wish to thank my wife, Estelle, for solving the many computer problems I encountered while working on this book, and for her many other forms of support.

The Art of Nonfiction

1

Preliminary Remarks

The first precondition of this course, and of any type of writing, is: do not get a sense of unearned guilt. If you have difficulty with writing, do not conclude that there is something wrong with you. Writing should never be a test of self-esteem. If things are not going as you want, do not see it as proof of an unknowable flaw in your subconscious.

Never take the blame for something you do *not* know. Be sure, however, to take the blame for writing errors you *do* know about. That much is open to your conscious mind, and pertains to how carefully you edit.

If you tell yourself you are guilty for not writing brilliant sentences within five minutes, that stops your subconscious and leads to a host of writing problems. Writing is not an index of psychological health. (Overconscientiousness is one reason a person might aspire to something too ambitious, and then blame himself if it does not come easily.) If you do have any guilt, earned or unearned, that is between you and your psychologist. When you sit down to write, however, you must regard yourself as perfect, omniscient, and omnipotent.

Of course, you are not omniscient and omnipotent; no human

skill, if at all interesting, can be perfect every time. Properly, therefore, you should feel that you have the capacity to write well, but that it is difficult. And you should not want an easy job—you do not want to be a hack—and therefore you should take all the trouble, and have all the patience, that writing requires. Do not conclude, at the first difficulty, that you are hopeless. This is the sense in which you must feel omniscient and omnipotent: not that everything you write will automatically be perfect, but that you have the capacity to make your work what you want to make it.

This leads to a second point. Contrary to all schools of art and esthetics, writing is something one can learn. There is no mystery about it.

In literature, as in all the fine arts, complex premises must be set early in a person's mind, so that a beginning adult may not have enough time to set them and thus cannot learn to write. Even these premises can be learned, theoretically, but the person would have to acquire them on his own. So I am inclined to say that fiction writing—and the fine arts in general—cannot be taught. Much of the technical skill involved can be, but not the essence.

However, any person who can speak English grammatically can learn to write nonfiction. Nonfiction writing is not difficult, though it is a technical skill. Its only difficulty pertains to a person's method of thinking or psycho-epistemology.[1] What you need for nonfiction writing is what you need for life in general: an orderly method of thinking. If you have problems in this regard, they will slow you down (in both realms). But writing is literally only the skill of putting down on paper a *clear* thought, in *clear* terms. Everything else, such as drama and "jazziness," is merely the trimmings.

I once said that the three most important elements of fiction are plot, plot, and plot. The equivalent in nonfiction is: *clarity, clarity,* and *clarity.*

---

[1] " 'Psycho-epistemology,' a term coined by Ayn Rand, pertains not to the content of a man's ideas, but to his method of awareness, i.e., the method by which his mind habitually deals with its content" (Leonard Peikoff, editor's footnote in Ayn Rand's *Philosophy: Who Needs It* [New York: New American Library, 1982]).

Harold Fleming, the author of *Ten Thousand Commandments*, once showed me a quotation he carried with him, from *The Education of Henry Adams*: "The result of a year's work depends more on what is struck out than on what is left in, on the sequence of the main lines of thought, than on their play and variety." Incidentally, there is not one extra word in this quotation. It is pruned down to the minimum necessary to express the thought. This is a fine way of making the point that clarity comes above all else. The first absolute is: be clear. Drama, jazziness, color—which can be added later—are never as important as clarity.

Nobody can learn to write without practicing, because there are so many subconscious integrations to be automatized. Nobody can write strictly by conscious effort. No matter how much theory you know, you will not be a good writer until you practice. Therefore, do not expect your first articles to be easy. They will be difficult, and as you develop they will become even more difficult, because you will attempt more ambitious themes. But in a different sense writing becomes easier: with each article you write you learn something, so that at the end of the article you are better than you were at the beginning.

How good you become depends on your premises and interests, and on how much time you devote to writing. But the skill *can* be learned. It is not mysterious and does not have to be torture.

Remember this point, particularly when you feel you will never write again or know what writing is. That sense of helplessness is inherent in struggling with a new thought. But any particular writing problem you might have is solvable (though, as in any introspection, it is not always easy to identify your problem). Writing is no more difficult a skill than any other, such as engineering. Like every human activity, it requires practice and knowledge. But there is nothing mystical to it.

The secret of writing is to be professional about it.

You can be professional before you publish anything—if you approach writing as a job. If you apply to writing the same standards and methods that people regularly apply to other professions, you will take a lot of weight off your subconscious and increase your productive capacity.

If you do not regard writing as a job, self-doubt will necessarily enter your mind, and you will be paralyzed. You will be putting yourself on trial every time you attempt to write. Instead of being an expression of your self-esteem, writing becomes its test. If so, it will be a miracle if you ever connect two sentences.

What does a person do in other professions when he feels self-doubt? If his approach is professional, he retains his knowledge of his own intelligence. He does not doubt his professional abilities, even though he may have difficulties to solve. He also understands that if he wants to advance, he has to expand his knowledge. The "If I don't get a raise there's something wrong with me" type of self-doubt is not relevant and does not enter his mind.

This same hard-headed, reality orientation is what you have to assume in regard to writing. I regard the piece of paper as my employer. I have to fill that piece of paper. How I feel—whether it is difficult or not, whether I am stuck or not—is irrelevant. It is as irrelevant as it would be if I were an employee of Hank Rearden [an industrialist in *Atlas Shrugged*]. He would not tolerate it if I told him, "I can't work today because I have self-doubt" or "I have a self-esteem crisis." Yet that is what most people do, in effect, when it comes to writing. I have always taken the professional approach. Of course, I can never guarantee how long some piece will take me, but my assignment is always to fill that page. I know a certain subject has to be stated, and I have the capacity to state it. What the difficulties are is irrelevant. They are my problem, and I will solve it.

My focus in this course is on writing articles, though much of what I say applies to books as well. Among articles, my focus is on the "middle range."

Nonfiction writing covers a wide range, from theoretical works that deal with broad, abstract principles, to concrete journalistic reporting. Theoretical articles discuss new fundamentals or present a new approach to issues on a fundamental level. (See, for example, Leonard Peikoff's "The Analytic-Synthetic Dichotomy."[2]) The proper medium for these articles is academic journals (except in

---

[2]Included in Ayn Rand, *Introduction to Objectivist Epistemology*, 2nd ed. (New York: New American Library, 1990).

the case of Objectivist articles, since no academic journal would publish them). Journalistic articles, on the other hand, consist not of theorizing, but of reporting on a given phenomenon or event—describing some concrete event or situation. (See, for example, Henry Kamm's "For Three Minutes I Felt Free."[3])

The articles I most enjoy writing are in the middle range.

Middle-range articles fall somewhere between theoretical and journalistic articles. They consist of the application of abstractions to concretes, which is what most intellectual magazines contain. Such articles deal neither with philosophical theory nor with concrete reporting. They accept a theoretical proposition and analyze some current event or some aspect of the culture from that viewpoint.

Two examples are Pope Paul VI's encyclical *Humanae Vitae*, and my reply to it, "On Living Death."[4] The Pope's encyclical is middle-range—actually, high middle-range—because he applies basic principles of Catholic philosophy and religion (concerning the sanctity of life, God's will, and a woman's duty) to narrower issues, namely love, marriage, and birth control. The idea of God's will, or the view that man may not interfere with natural processes, is a theoretical subject; but it is applied here to such issues as what man should do in marriage. In my reply, I do not state any new Objectivist theory; I discuss why the Pope's theories are wrong from the Objectivist viewpoint. I apply my view of human rights, the nature of love, and the nature of marriage to the issues raised in this encyclical. That is writing in the middle range.

If I wrote a critique of Kant, and in the process I defined some new theory,[5] that would be a theoretical article. But if I simply took an aspect of his philosophy and showed why it is wrong according to Objectivism, that would be middle range.

---

[3] *The New York Times*, October 13, 1968; reprinted alongside Ayn Rand's "The 'Inexplicable Personal Alchemy'" in Ayn Rand, *Return of the Primitive: The Anti-Industrial Revolution*, edited, with additional essays, by Peter Schwartz (New York: Meridian, 1999).

[4] Ayn Rand, *The Voice of Reason: Essays in Objectivist Thought*, edited, with additional essays by Leonard Peikoff (New York: New American Library, 1989).

[5] For example, see Ayn Rand, "Causality Versus Duty," *Philosophy: Who Needs It*.

Theoretical articles, written to present something fundamental and new, are the most valuable. But you should not aim for them. You should not wait to discover something new in order to write.

No matter what you write, however, a knowledge of the principles of writing is invaluable. But what you do not know consciously is not really knowledge. If you do not know certain principles of thinking and writing explicitly, you are helpless to use them. You may practice these principles without knowing it (like the man in Molière's comedy who did not know he was talking prose); but they are not in your control if you have never conceptualized them.

The present course should help you immensely with this task. This does not mean that inspiration will come to you automatically. But it does mean that you will know how to make it come when you need it.

2

Choosing a
Subject and Theme

Whenever you have a problem, whether you are writing an article or building a doghouse, do not look *inside* for the solution. Do not ask: "How do *I* do it? Why don't *I* know it?" Look *outside* and ask: "What is the *nature* of the thing I want to do?"

What is the nature of an article? First observe that you cannot do everything at once. Whatever you are writing—a theoretical work on a revolutionary idea or a small piece about a narrow concrete—you cannot say everything you know about the subject. You must accept this premise fully, so that it becomes part of your subconscious and operates automatically. You can do this by asking yourself whether you always knew everything you know today. Obviously you did not. Knowledge is acquired in steps.

Good teachers recognize that you cannot teach everything at once, which is why a four-year course of study must be divided into semesters, and semesters into individual lectures. But when it comes to writing, people forget this principle and attempt to cram everything they know about the subject into one article. Yet this cannot be done even in a series of *books*. Since every item of knowledge is connected to every other, and since there is only one reality, if you wanted to present an exhaustive case on any one subject, you would have to write the work of a universal scholar. For example, you would start with an article on the New York theater, and would end up covering science, epistemology, metaphysics, psychology, etc.

All writing is *selective* in every aspect—not only in its style, but in its most basic content, because you cannot communicate everything.

(However, I prefer the person who tries to write everything in one article—which at least reveals a good intention—to the concrete-bound writer who discusses only the toes of a statue, or to the linguistic analyst who can write only about the ten uses of the word "but." So if you are overambitious, I sympathize with you; nevertheless, this approach is disastrous.)

You must delimit your subject and theme.

Some people commit the error of trying to present all they know by writing an *unanswerable* article. This is a mistake on at least two counts. First, it is impossible, because if the theme is important, it would take a book to *prove* it. In an article, you do not prove your theme, you *demonstrate* it. These are almost synonymous, but here is the distinction. "Proof" applies mainly to theoretical subjects. But when you write about merely an aspect of a subject, such as a cultural or philosophical issue that is part of a cluster of issues, you do not try to prove some point. That would require a much broader and longer piece. Instead, you demonstrate your point, i.e., present it and *indicate* its proof (which is not the same as giving the proof). For example, in my article "The 'Inexplicable Personal Alchemy,'"[1] I do not prove that we should treat the men of reason better—I merely provide the material for such a proof. I demonstrate that the policy of destroying the young because of their virtues is disastrous, and I show its results in two extreme cases: Russia and America. But to actually prove this, I would have to prove the validity and importance of reason. Here, for an Objectivist audience, I take that premise as axiomatic. (The article is still of value to a non-Objectivist. It will not prove the point to him, but if he is interested, it will jolt him

---

[1]Her article was a reaction to Henry Kamm's 1968 article "For Three Minutes I Felt Free," which covered some protesters in Soviet Russia. She contrasts young, pro-reason dissidents in Russia with the anti-reason hippies in America.

into investigating further the issue of reason versus irrationality. And I present my point in such a way that the worst irrationalist would not dare say openly that he is opposed to those Russian protesters and is in favor of the hippies.)

The second reason why trying to write an unanswerable article is a mistake is that the author is assuming his readers do not possess free will. He is assuming he must present, by some undefined means, a case that no one could resist. But clearly such an assumption is false. People can evade the most obvious logical connections. Therefore, if you try to write such an article, you are defeated at the outset, because you are asking the impossible of yourself. As a result, either you will be unable to write (and will not know why), or you will write endlessly, following sidelines, each of which leads to further sidelines. Instead of being unanswerable, you will raise more questions than you answer. (This is an eloquent illustration of the fact that acting on a wrong premise achieves the opposite of your intention.)

If the unanswerable or exhaustive article is impossible, what kind is possible? An article, by its nature, must treat a severely delimited *aspect* of a subject, not a whole subject.

The standard of measurement here is relative, but I mean a "whole subject" in its most basic sense. For instance, if your subject is political, then the whole subject is politics, with all its key aspects. That would be a proper subject for a book, but not for an article. Even in writing a book, you would have to delimit what politics is: you cannot include too much metaphysics, epistemology, or ethics, even though each is relevant. In a book, you indicate your framework, delimit your subject, and stick to essentials. So, obviously, any large-scale subject cannot be the focus of an article. (Actually, my *Introduction to Objectivist Epistemology*[2] does not qualify as an article. It is really a monograph, which is why I had to write it in the form of eight installments—much too long even for a theoretical article. It should have been published originally as a book. This is a good illustration of the form an article should *not* take.)

[2]Originally published in installments in *The Objectivist* (July 1966–February 1967).

Consider my article "On Living Death,"[3] which deals with birth control. I do not treat the whole issue, only the Objectivist critique of the Catholic position. Further, I do not cover all the relevant Catholic literature, only one papal encyclical. Even though I deal with fundamentals, my subject is only one aspect of a broad issue.

A useful exercise is to look at some good articles and name the broader subject and the particular aspect each treats. You will find that the subject always deals with a partial aspect examined from some viewpoint; it is never a crammed condensation of the whole.

Once you recognize the nature of an article, the next step is to decide on an article of your own. Observe that there are two essential elements of an article: subject and theme. The *subject* is what the article is about: the issue, event, or person it deals with. (Again, an article must cover only an aspect of a whole.) The *theme* is what the author wants to say about the subject—what he brings to the subject. If the article is in the middle range, he brings his evaluation of the subject; if it is theoretical, he brings his new idea.

Consider a middle-range approach to the subject of modern theater. You could write many articles on this, and thus write on the same subject but with different themes. For example, one person could write on modern theater as an indication of cultural disintegration, while some modernist might try to show why he thinks it is good, or what its social significance is. There are many potential approaches to the same subject.

As for theoretical works, consider my *Introduction to Objectivist Epistemology*. The subject is epistemology (and more narrowly the nature of concepts), and the theme is my theory of concepts. Or: the subject of my article "The Psycho-epistemology of Art"[4] is art, and the theme is my definition of the nature, purpose, and source of art. In theoretical articles, the theme is the abstract point the author wants to make. It does not include an evaluation.

The easiest way to identify your subject and theme is to ask yourself why you want to write the article. The more clearly you state

---

[3] *The Voice of Reason*.

[4] Ayn Rand, *The Romantic Manifesto* (New York: New American Library, 1975).

your answer, the easier it will be to create your outline and write your article.

The question "Why do I want to write this article?" involves two sub-questions: "What subject do I want to write about?" and "What do I want to say about the subject—i.e., what is my theme?" In answering these questions, you may discover that your reasons are inappropriate. For example, you find that you want to write an article because you are angry at the president. That is not yet a good reason. Writing is not occupational therapy. The next question should be: "Is there a wider reason I feel so angry?" If you have a valid reason, and nobody has yet taken your particular approach to the president, then your article turns from a vague, subjective emotion into a potentially valuable piece.

As an example of selecting a subject and theme, consider again my 1969 article "The 'Inexplicable Personal Alchemy.'"[5] I felt a strong emotion when I read Kamm's piece about the young Russian rebels. I asked my husband whether he had read it, and he had. His reaction was the same, but without the personal details. He thought it was beautiful and possessed grandeur, and that there was something very tragic about it. That was the first clue that my reaction was not totally subjective, i.e., based on mere personal history.

My next questions were: "Is there a wider meaning to this feeling? Why do I feel such pain?" Immediately I knew the reason: Kamm's article portrays the destruction of the best of the young. What is so tragic here is that they are idealists in a hopeless situation, and yet they are still trying to fight their destroyers. The next questions I asked were: "Why are they still fighting? Why do I feel their situation is tragic?" I saw that they are fighting on the basis of their virtues, which they are too young to identify. They are doomed, yet it is the best within them that makes them act as they do, without their even knowing fully why.

This was my reaction to the destruction of young people in Russia. So far, it is a narrow subject, of interest in a specialized study of Russia, but not yet appropriate for an American article. But the next

---

[5]In what follows it is important to keep in mind that Ayn Rand was born in Czarist Russia (in 1905) and left Soviet Russia in the twenties.

connection in my mind was that this phenomenon is not exclusive to Russia. Young people are being destroyed for their virtues and for their devotion to ideas in this country too—in our colleges.

My next thought was that the American hippies are the exact opposite of those young Russians. In Russia, they are fighting and dying for freedom of the mind; here they are parading naked in theaters and destroying universities in the name of freedom *from* the mind. At this point, I knew I had an article.

I have described this process in slow motion; in reality, it did not take me more than five minutes. The connections fell into place because my subconscious holds a standing order to be on the lookout for article themes.

The subject of my article, therefore, is the destruction of the best among the young. The theme is that this is a terrible crime, and that American hippies and their admiring educators are even guiltier than the brutes in Russia. Note that the form of the article and the amount of commentary were determined by the subject. I had to analyze the meaning of a certain event in Russia—the destruction of young idealists—on the basis of a brief, journalistic description provided in the *Times* article. Then I had to present the American hippies in the same terms, i.e., by concrete dramatizations. In contrast to my article on the student rebellion,[6] this is not a theoretical discussion of what is wrong with the so-called vanguard of American youth. It is a concretized presentation, through highly selective attributes, of the contrast between the Russian and American rebels. Once my subject and theme were clear, everything else fell into place. Had I not defined the theme, but merely started by saying "I feel strongly about Russia, let me write something," I would have been in trouble.

Now, I could have written a different article on the same Kamm piece, e.g., an article on the evil of communism. Here the subject is the same, but the theme is a denunciation of Russia's treatment of the young. Or the theme could be a denunciation of Russian censorship. Or the evil of cultural exchanges, and other forms of

[6]"The Cashing-in: The Student 'Rebellion,'" in *Capitalism: The Unknown Ideal* (New York: New American Library, 1967).

American cooperation with Russia. I could name many aspects from which good articles could be written, all based on Kamm's report. There are as many possibilities as there are professions: a historian could focus on the subject from one perspective, a philosopher from another, an economist from yet another.

There are no rules for selecting a theme, provided it is of broad interest. For example, if upon reading Kamm's piece someone decided to focus his theme on Russian streets (which Kamm mentions) and how unsanitary they are, that would not be valid. It is too narrow. When you see a crime like the destruction of young idealists because of their virtues, you should not focus on puny details. That destroys the significance of the subject by undermining its seriousness, and by not featuring it. Such a theme is irrelevant to, and thus clashes with, the subject. Your subject and theme must be commensurate.

Noteworthy here is a cover from an early issue of *The New Yorker*. It pictured the wall of a museum, upon which hung a large painting of a very savage caveman. He is running through the jungle carrying a naked woman, who is screaming. He is leering ferociously, and obviously intends to rape her. As he runs through the jungle, he is breaking the branches he encounters, and doves fly off to avoid him. In the museum, in front of this painting, sits a little old lady with an easel, copying the painting. But out of all of this violent subject matter, she chooses to copy only the flight of doves. This is a good visual example of selecting a theme too small for the subject.

You should not select a theme which is too big, either. If you choose a minuscule event and try to build a broad theme around it, you will end up with floating abstractions [i.e., abstractions not connected to reality], since your subject gives you insufficient material for that broad an approach.

Of course, you must first select your subject and then your theme, because anything you choose to write must be about *something*, and you must establish what that is before you can determine what you want to say about it. In writing fiction, where the equivalent of the subject is the plot, you can start by thinking about the theme—or any other aspect of the novel. But with nonfiction, you must start with the subject. (When you are experienced, the process is automatized, so that you get your subject and theme virtually together and at once. But there are actually two selections.)

Incidentally, there is no such thing as *the* best theme. It is disastrous to write with the idea that you must make your article "the best possible" on a given subject. Since you are treating only one aspect of a subject, there are as many other aspects—giving rise to as many themes—as there are, say, professions. Just as you cannot say one valid profession is better than another, so you cannot say one aspect of a subject is objectively superior to another.

You *can* establish a certain hierarchy of fundamentality. For instance, to treat an enduring, philosophical aspect of a subject is more fundamental than to treat a transient, journalistic aspect. But this is a very loose hierarchy, because there can be a bad article with too broad a theme, and a valuable one with an enlightening, albeit narrower, theme.

Your only concern should be rationally justifying *your* approach, i.e., explaining to yourself, and to anyone who asks, why what you have to say is valuable to the reader. One practical consequence of this principle is that you do not start with a Kantian, or mystical, idea of value—by which you seek the "best" approach in a metaphysical vacuum.

The decisive element here is your own hierarchy of intellectual values: what subject interests you and what you want to say about it. Your standard should be the best approach that *you* want to take. As long as your value premises are rational, the hierarchy is established by what *you* find important. Thus, the directive you give yourself should be: do not choose a lesser aspect than the deepest one that interests you and that you can do. For instance, in response to the Kamm piece, it would be improper to decide that while you could write a good article on the Soviet educational system—which interests you—you will instead write an easy article about Soviet mothers, because it requires less time for research. That is not a valid reason. The latter article would not be good, because it would bore *you*, and therefore would not be interesting or convincing to your readers.

I do not mean that if a theme of interest to you requires a lot of research, you should do it even though you cannot afford the time.

If your article requires that much research, then the theme is somewhat outside your present knowledge and interest. It would be too broad a theme for *your* hierarchy. The point is: take the widest theme you can handle, given your knowledge and interests.

If you find you have nothing *new* to say about your subject, do not write that article. This is a crucial point that many people, especially beginners, fail to recognize. A young man once showed me an article he had written on capitalism, which was an utter rehash. When I asked him whether this had been said before, he replied that it had. And that was the problem. He wanted to say something in favor of capitalism—but he had nothing new to say about it.

If you have nothing new to say, no matter how brilliantly you can say it, do not do it. An article stands or falls on its subject and theme. Those "brilliant" essays that say nothing (which *The New Yorker* is full of) are mere finger exercises and a waste of developed style.

"New" here does not mean totally unprecedented. It does not require a fundamental philosophical principle never heard of before. Since an article deals with partial aspects of a subject, the novelty of your theme need not be world-shaking. But your idea must be new in the context of that subject. For example, *The Objectivist* recently published a good article on government control of the arts. Government controls are not new; but, to my knowledge, nobody had previously demonstrated how wrong it is for the government to go into the arts, and how it succeeded by default. This idea is not new from the point of view of the relationship between government and the economy; but it is with regard to the history of a particular aspect of the American economy, namely the arts.

On a related point, some people think an article, to be new, must do more than "simply" apply some basic principle to a new situation. On this view, since I have written on the student rebellion at Berkeley,[7] for example, anything I might write on the rebellion at Cornell would be a rehash. But if that were true, you could not write middle-range articles, only theoretical ones. In fact, you can legitimately apply the same principles to different concretes and stress different

[7]"The Cashing-in: The Student 'Rebellion.' "

aspects, and thereby write a hundred articles, none of them a rehash. There is no limit to how many aspects of a subject you can handle without repeating yourself. You could apply the same principles I used in my article on Berkeley to the situation at Cornell, and stress, say, the attitude of the moderates or the degree to which force has escalated since Berkeley. These would be original articles. (I would not write such articles, because once I have written on a subject it usually bores *me* to return to it; but that does not mean it is not a valid article for someone else.) Applying philosophy to reality is not automatic. To show how certain ideas apply to current events takes a new mental effort each time, and is therefore a value to your audience.

In a sense, I have said nothing new since *We the Living*.[8] Of course, there are many new ideas in *Atlas Shrugged*, but you *could* say, broadly speaking, that the ideas were all implicit in *We the Living*; after all, I was for selfishness and individual rights in both books. If your standard of the new is too broad, ultimately you would have to say: "Nobody has stated anything new since Aristotle said A is A, because you cannot go beneath the Law of Identity, nor say anything without it. We are all only elaborating on it." But that is not the proper standard of novelty. (On the other hand, paraphrase is not enough. If someone says, "The government should not impose so many controls," and in the name of novelty you write, "The government should not impose that great a number of controls," obviously that would *not* constitute novelty.)

Judge the novelty of your theme by asking yourself whether you have seen this view expressed before. If you know the subject and have not come across this approach (and you need not know everything written on the subject), then what you have to say is new.

In sum, there are three questions to ask yourself before you write an article: "What do I want to write about?" "What do I want to say about that subject?" and "What is the element of novelty in my theme?"

You should write down these questions and your answers. This is

---

[8]Ayn Rand's first novel, published by Macmillan in 1936 (rev. ed., Random House, 1959; 60th anniversary ed., Dutton, 1995).

especially important in the beginning, before you have automatized the process of selecting a subject and theme. In writing out your answers, make them objective. If you cannot write something down clearly and objectively, then you do not really know it. Any vagueness or indecision on any fundamental aspect of your article will be disastrous. That which you cannot name you know only approximately.

The great majority of writing problems come from approximations in one's mind. The subconscious does not work through approximations. It is more absolutist than your conscious mind—though it is a good idea to try to make *that* absolutist as well, in the sense of being very precise in your conscious decisions.

3

Judging One's Audience

Once you decide on a subject and theme and determine that your idea is new, ask yourself why someone else should be interested in your article. This will lend objectivity to your selection of a theme. I illustrated this process when I discussed "The 'Inexplicable Personal Alchemy' " (see pp. 11–13). So long as I regarded Kamm's piece as being of special interest only to *me* (given my history), that interest was subjective, and I would not be justified in writing an article about it. But once I concluded that every educated layman should be interested in how the best of the young are being destroyed because of their loyalty to reason, my theme became objectively valid.

Judging your audience is a subdivision of the topic covered [in chapter 2]. It applies, however, not only to choosing a subject and theme, but also to making an outline and to your actual writing. I will now cover the relevant principles which you need to understand and automatize.

Judging your audience is a complicated issue. But its very complexity eliminates the need for detailed rules. You cannot estimate your audience with precision, because there are as many different audiences as there are individuals. No two readers will be exactly alike or have the same psycho-epistemology. But you need to know the general category of person involved. Just as there must be no vagueness in your mind about your subject, theme, or outline, so too with respect to your readers. You have to identify, on paper and in objective terms, what type of audience you are addressing.

Actually, you make this kind of judgment constantly in talking to people. For instance, you do not speak to children the way you do to your peers, and you talk to your boss or people more knowledgeable than you in yet another way. You do not change your ideas, or talk up or down, but you are aware of their state of knowledge in comparison with yours. In writing, what you must primarily judge is your readers' knowledge, because that determines how much you need to explain.

For example, if an Objectivist writes for an Objectivist audience, he need not prove every Objectivist principle he refers to. And if he writes for a general audience, he cannot prove the whole of Objectivism in one article. But in the latter case, he would need to clarify certain principles more than he would in the former.

Consider my one-page article on the Apollo 8 astronauts reading the Bible from space.[1] I could not, in a page, tell the reader why reason is superior to faith, and why I object to the Bible. I took such knowledge for granted. I could do that in an Objectivist publication, and (conceivably) in a liberal publication like *The New York Times*. But it would have been improper to write it that way for a small-town newspaper in the Bible Belt. Even with the best intentions, the majority of those readers could not understand the article. Their intellectual framework is totally different.

This is how you project the reader's frame of reference, without which you cannot start an article. You assume some level of knowledge—some context—which *you* cannot teach your readers, but must take as the base from which you write. That is a requirement of objectivity.

Incidentally, if you write for a young audience, never write down. The only difference your estimate of an audience should make is in

[1]"Brief Comments," *The Objectivist*, November 1968 (Gaylordsville, CT: Second Renaissance Books, 1990).

how much complexity and abstraction you can convey and how much explanation is necessary.

How do you judge an audience's knowledge? Assume you are writing for Objectivists. (The principles are the same for any audience.) First identify the necessary context. Say you are writing an article on government interference in the arts. You know that if you start explaining what art and government are, you will never get to the subject. You have to assume the audience knows what they are. What you *are* telling them about is, say, how the government entered the field of art, the arguments offered in favor of this interference, and the incorrectness of these arguments. You must ask yourself at each step—in stating the theme, making the outline, and writing—what *you* needed to know to write this article. At one time you did *not* know by what steps the government entered this field. How did you learn it? You read a great deal about it, for instance, which convinced you that the government entered the field by default, and that its proponents used false arguments. Well, *this* is what you want to communicate to your audience. If you assume that your readers already know the whole history, then you have not chosen a proper subject and theme. But if they do not know it, then your choice is appropriate.

To be interested in this subject, an Objectivist reader needs to know the general impropriety of government interference. You need not *prove* this to him. You can assume it as your context, though you must refer to that knowledge when necessary.

Many writers make the mistake of being neutral about their audience's context. For example, an author knows that his audience holds a certain viewpoint, yet he writes as if the audience were neutral. He ignores the prior context of knowledge *he* needed in order to begin to write the article and falsely concludes that his audience lacks it too. This can create confusion in the reader's mind. On the other hand, suppose that because *you* know Hubert Humphrey was a proponent of government interference in the arts, you decide this fact is self-evident and refer to his bad influence without ever citing his views. That too would be ignoring the nature of your audience's knowledge. To denounce Humphrey, you must inform your readers of his involvement, since you are enlightening them about the history of this kind of government interference. Do not assume they know his role in it.

For every part of your article, know what your context is and whether your readers have it too. *Ask yourself what you can omit and of what you must inform them.* This is how you reach an accurate judgment of what you need to tell your readers. Incidentally, it is always safer (at least on the first draft) to overexplain than to underexplain. When in doubt, include the information, because in editing you can always shorten or eliminate the passage.

An important principle here is that man is born *tabula rasa.* Writers often assume something is self-evident, since they themselves now take it for granted, when in fact it is complex. *Nothing* is self-evident except the evidence of your senses. Therefore, when you write, assume nothing is self-evident but logic. (Logic is actually not self-evident, but in order to communicate, you must assume a person knows how to make logical connections.) For the rest, since no knowledge exists at birth, you must judge what acquired knowledge is necessary to make your point understandable—and then you must communicate it.

A corollary issue is that when your subject is controversial, you must take cognizance of any prevalent errors. This is not an issue of whether people agree with you or not, but of recognizing that if certain errors are widespread in a culture, your best readers may not know how your views apply to those issues. For example, in *Introduction to Objectivist Epistemology*, at the end of each chapter I refer to some current error to indicate how my position applies. In chapter 4, for instance, when I finish my discussion of measurement, I mention psychologists who measure kneejerks rather than deal with psychological principles, and mystics who object to *anything* important being measurable. Never assume your readers will make such connections automatically, particularly if you are presenting something new. Of course, you cannot cover every implication, but you can indicate the leading ones.

But make sure, in touching on these errors, that you are not misunderstood. In dealing with an issue on which your position is different from the commonly held view, you must have enough space to make your point fully clear. If you do not, it is better to omit the topic entirely. The mistake beginners often make, in writing about a subject which they can present very clearly, is to bring in some controversial issue in passing, perhaps as an example. This only creates confusion. I do not mean that you should not raise such issues—only that you should not do so as a sideline, when you are unable to present your full viewpoint clearly.

Whether you write for an Objectivist publication or for *TV Guide*, you must judge how much your audience knows. But always address yourself to the *best* of that audience.

A "type of audience" is an abstraction. Concretely, you will find evaders and people with dreadful psycho-epistemologies in any audience (including an Objectivist one). The cognitive level of your readers does not determine their psycho-epistemology. Children can make a more intelligent, better focused audience than professors. Therefore, do not give any consideration whatever to the possibility of *bad* psycho-epistemologies. Once you have projected your audience's level of knowledge, address yourself to the best, most focused mind that you can imagine in that cognitive group.

It is improper to address yourself to a faulty psycho-epistemology. Devising a rational method to address the irrational is a contradiction. If some of your readers are irrational, there are no principles by which to decide what they will choose to hear, what they will not, and what connections they will make. Neither you nor the evader can predict what he will miss and what he will integrate. That is in the nature of irrationality.

So do not psychologize. Do not make allowances for readers' mental weaknesses. For example, do not tell yourself: "I'm saying something new or antagonistic—how can I prevent their minds from closing? How can I soften the blow?" If you ask such questions, you will only paralyze your own mind by attempting the impossible. You cannot reach a mind that chooses to be closed or is so incapacitated that even if, momentarily, it wanted to integrate properly, it could not. Such a mind lacks the capacity of full focus, and is the proper concern only of a psychotherapist. In all dealings with people, you have to deal with their conscious minds.

In writing, assume *full rationality*. Assume your audience is at its best and that you have to live up to it. That is, establish your general view of the audience, and then proceed as if you were writing to yourself as a member of that audience—at your best, most perceptive potential. You must project the most cognitively severe mind—and the only mind that you can project completely is your own at its most consistent, clearest level of functioning. In that sense, write as if you are trying to convince yourself.

To achieve objectivity and clarity, ask yourself how you would make something clear to a person as severe as you are. Project the process by which you would convince yourself. Assume you do not know your material and must discover it from the article alone. Be as rigorous as if your article were written by a stranger. If you are not—if there are faults in your thinking—it will be reflected in your writing. (This is one way writing helps your psycho-epistemology, and vice versa. The better your psycho-epistemology, the easier writing will be.)

This process is the *opposite* of subjectivism; and it is a difficult responsibility, because you might easily think: "If I write for myself, I know what I want to say, and therefore anything I write will be clear to me even from a few shorthand notes." But what is required in writing is strict objectivity. That is why I said you must write to yourself *as if you did not know the subject.*

Use your own psychology as a reader to guide yourself as a writer. When questions occur to you, your best reference, if you are objective, is yourself. The ability to switch perspective between that of the writer and that of the reader (of the finished product), is the best training in objectivity. It is also good training in editing—whether your own work or that of others. Switching perspective helps, because there are so many problems in writing, and you may be so overwhelmed by the number of considerations, that you can lose your ability to judge your work. It is helpful in this situation to step back and ask: "How would *I* judge it if I were reading it?" This clears your mental circuits of all the unresolved complexities of writing, and gives you a fresh perspective as a reader.

For example, if you hesitate about whether to include a particular detail, the ultimate judge should be you as a reader, because there are no absolute rules in such a case applicable to every article.

Switch perspective, pretend not to know the subject, and ask yourself whether you would find the detail clarifying. Take your own answer, if it is objective, as your standard. By "objective" I mean that you can give yourself at least one good reason why you prefer to keep the detail or omit it. ("I don't know why, but I feel like keeping it" does not qualify.) After all, your article is written within the context of your own psycho-epistemology and your own knowledge. Appealing to yourself as a reader produces a consistent, reliable standard of judgment for the whole article. If your article is to be well-integrated, the ultimate judge of what is appropriate and why has to be you.

Connected to the issue of judging an audience is the issue of knowing what you want your audience to do with your article. Or to put it another way: do not have several purposes—and several audiences—in mind simultaneously. Be clear on this issue, because subconsciously it will affect your whole article.

Every *general-interest* article is written for one purpose: to communicate knowledge to the intelligent layman. You might have a different purpose—say, urging your audience to take some action; but if so, the entire article must be written differently, as a professional article addressed to your colleagues. But you cannot write for your colleagues and for a general lay audience at the same time. If you try to combine the two types of audiences and purposes, you will be giving information to laymen and simultaneously telling your colleagues how to put this information into practice. Your article will contain contradictions in practically every paragraph and will fall apart.

For instance, if you write a general article about the methodology of education, you do it differently than if you were addressing teachers. A lay audience has comparatively little knowledge of the subject, and has merely a general interest in those principles it can apply to its own dealings with education. Members of a general audience would be interested in knowing, for example, how the Objectivist method differs from Dewey's. Thus you would show that according to the Objectivist method, teachers need to appeal to principles and concretize them with examples, whereas Dewey's method is concrete-bound and avoids principles and integration.

But teachers have a different level of motivation and interest, as well as a higher level of technicality. If you were writing for them, you would have to provide technical details concerning how to achieve certain effects. You would discuss what type of exercises to give the class, what kinds of errors to look for, in what way the remnants of Deweyite education will interfere with the class's understanding, what to do as an antidote, etc. The "how-to" approach is appropriate for the professional. But that is of no interest to the layman. It is almost the difference between theoretical science for the layman—and applied technology for the professional. The *purpose* for which you write depends on your audience.

In most of my articles I *do* have an action-conclusion, but only in very generalized terms. For instance, the purpose of "America's Persecuted Minority: Big Business"[2] was to inform the audience about the nature of our antitrust laws. It is a general enlightenment article. So I give some examples, describe their history, and show why they are wrong. In the conclusion I say we should advocate the revision, and eventual repeal, of antitrust—especially the imprisonment provision. But I am not teaching the audience how to fight antitrust; I am merely indicating a positive direction, after having exposed a dreadful negative. Since this is a negative trend which is becoming worse, it is appropriate to indicate (without going into details) that some kind of action is possible. But if I expanded my conclusion and said the reader should gather the members of his community opposed to antitrust and should communicate with me, because I am forming a committee, that would be improper; it would belong in an action-article. If my purpose is the organization of such a committee, then I must write the article differently. I must briefly summarize what is wrong with antitrust (assuming a greater level of knowledge in my audience) and concentrate, not on the history, but on rousing people to action and indicating what they can do. This type of action-article is called a manifesto. Nothing is wrong with a manifesto *per se*, though you must know when it is appropriate. But do not confuse a manifesto with a general-information article.

General articles are of interest to *all* readers because they are

[2]*Capitalism: The Unknown Ideal* (New York: New American Library, 1967).

usually written on a graded principle. A specialist will get much more from such an article than a general reader, but the general reader should get something worthwhile. To each according to his ability—or rather, according to his knowledge. If an article is clear, then each person gets out of it what he objectively brings to it, namely, that which he already understands. And if the article is good, and the reader has an active mind, it might stimulate him to inquire further about the aspects he does not understand or know about. That is not the article's purpose, but it is a fringe benefit of a good article.

Since many subjects can be treated in more than one way, if you do not clearly identify your audience, you may be strongly tempted to write more than one kind of article simultaneously. Whatever type of article you choose to write, you must decide—at the stage of selecting the subject and theme—who your readers are and thus what you intend to communicate to them.

4

Applying Philosophy
Without Preaching It

A problem many young writers suffer from, in various degrees, is the belief that an article should be propaganda—that it should preach one's philosophy. This is not merely a writing problem, so I will start with the broader philosophical issue involved in this error.

First, you need to grasp that there is no such *thing* as Objectivism or any other philosophy. Philosophy is the study of the fundamental nature of reality. "Fundamental" refers to a principle or truth which is present in a vast number of concretes. To say something is fundamental means that many other truths depend on it. To say philosophy studies the fundamentals of reality means it studies those facts present in, and those principles applicable to, everything that exists.

Every abstraction, and thus every principle, is manifested in an incalculable number of concretes. It is what the concretes have in common—*but it does not exist apart from them*. An abstraction is a form of human classification by which man integrates the evidence provided by his senses. Man rises above the perceptual level by integrating his percepts into concepts, his concepts into principles, his principles into sciences, and all of his sciences into a philosophy. Abstractions are objective, i.e., based on reality. But abstractions, including simple concepts of concretes, do not exist as such. What exists is only the material from which a concept is drawn.[1]

I have often said that the whole history of philosophy is a duel between Plato and Aristotle, and that this conflict is present in every issue.[2] If you think principles, and therefore philosophy, exist apart from concretes, then you are a Platonist. Plato believed abstractions are archetypes or universals that exist in some other realm, in the form of nonmaterial, supernatural entities. Now the deepest thing Objectivism has in common with Aristotle—and it has many things in common—is this: Aristotle was the first to grasp what most people still do not, namely, that everything that exists is a specific, concrete entity, or an aspect of one, such as an action of an entity, an attribute of an entity, a relationship it bears, etc. But the base of everything is an entity—not an idea or abstraction. An abstraction is the form in which we organize these entities in order to understand them.

To be an Aristotelian all the way down, you must grasp that only *concrete* events, *concrete* relationships, *concrete* problems exist. (If you are not Aristotelian all the way down, it is no moral crime; but it will cause problems, so train yourself to be one.) For example, the same abstract problem may exist in different parts of the world, and involve different people. But in each case, it is a concrete problem. Just as the abstraction "table" involves all the tables that exist—past, present, and future—so the abstract problem "man versus the state" has occurred in practically every society in history. It is the major political problem in the world today, but it is not a floating abstraction. It is an abstraction of relationships between man and a political system, and those relationships exist only in concrete forms. They exist in Russia, in Germany, in the United States—there is man against the state in Russia, in Germany, in America. But the mere fact that they are covered by the same abstraction does not

[1]For a fuller account of Ayn Rand's theory of concept formation, see her *Introduction to Objectivist Epistemology.*
[2]For example, see the title essay to Ayn Rand, *For the New Intellectual.* See also the epilogue ("The Duel Between Plato and Aristotle") to Leonard Peikoff, *Objectivism: The Philosophy of Ayn Rand* (New York: Dutton, 1991).

change the fact that they are separate concretes. The abstraction in-volves particular men, in particular situations, facing particular governments. There is no such thing as "man versus the state" in another, Platonic dimension.

When you are clear on this subject, you will be at home with abstractions. If you are not, the immediate danger is that you will be concrete-bound in your actual life, and indulge in floating abstractions in your philosophical convictions. Until men become fully Aristotelian, they cannot apply their philosophical principles to their own lives and actions. So on the one hand, they may have a complex, ivory-tower philosophy, and on the other, nevertheless act like savages.

Objectivists would not make such a crude mistake, but every mistake can be committed across a continuum of degrees. So although an Objectivist would not profess Objectivism and join the Communist Party, he might nevertheless accept the idea that his professed philosophical convictions exist in one department, and his daily life, judgments, and views in quite another.

The root of this mistake is that often, when a person accepts certain convictions, he does not integrate them thoroughly to the concretes he encounters. One need not think an entire issue over again each time it comes up. A thorough integration permits a person to recognize quickly when certain convictions of his apply to some concrete fact; only in complex situations does he have to do fresh thinking. Nevertheless, no matter how complex or simple it is, you must deal with every issue in your life according to your philosophy, and you cannot hold your philosophy "somewhere," apart from your daily actions.

If men could live by the range of the moment—by a concrete-bound method—we would not need philosophy. The purpose of philosophy is to guide a man in the course of his life. Unfortunately, many Objectivists have not fully accepted, concretized, and integrated this principle. For example, in the presence of a given event, work of art, person, etc., too many Objectivists ask themselves, "What do I *have* to feel?" instead of, "What *do* I feel?" And if they need to judge a situation which I have not discussed before, their approach is, "What *should* I think?" instead of, "What *do* I think?" This is the childhood remnant of anyone who to some extent was influenced either by the religion of the culture or, later in college, by Platonism. Both give the impression that the good, the important, the philosophical are like church on Sunday: you use them on special occasions, but they have nothing to do with daily life. If any part of this attitude remains in you, it is important to eliminate it.

Philosophy does not tell you concretely what to feel or think; it tells you what is true and right. If you have to judge something (e.g., a work of art, a government policy, a personal relationship), your philosophy gives you the right principles by which to judge it (if your philosophy is rational). Philosophy provides you with a criterion—but cannot apply it for you. In judging anything or anyone, *you* must decide whether it or he is good or bad.

Philosophy cannot give you a set of dogmas to be applied automatically. Religion does that—and unsuccessfully. The dogmatic Objectivist desperately tries to reduce principles to concrete rules that can be applied automatically, like a ritual, so as to bypass the responsibility of thinking and of moral analysis. These are "Objectivist" ritualists. They want Objectivism to give them what a religion promises, namely, ten or one hundred commandments, which they can apply without having to think about or judge anything.

Which philosophy is right is a separate inquiry. To discover the right one is the purpose of studying philosophy. But once you have convinced yourself that a given philosophy is right—that it corresponds to reality—you are armed only with a key, which will tell you by what criteria to judge a given event or person or choice—or article. But the concretes must be judged, evaluated, and organized *by you.*

Now, how does what I have said apply to writing? (I am here concerned primarily with middle-range articles, which apply philosophy to concretes.) Until a writer is fully Aristotelian, he will be unable properly to apply his philosophical principles to writing. When you write a middle-range article, the proper approach is to ask: "What do *I* think of this subject?" "What do *I* want to say?" If you doubt whether what you want to say is correct, that is a separate issue and has nothing to do with your article. If you have such doubts, put your article aside and do some additional thinking. But do not approach an article without a clear idea of your own evaluation of the subject. Do not try to muddle through in a state that is partly your own evaluation and partly a ritualistic application of Objectivist "bromides."

I next want to discuss two errors that tend to be committed by those who are not fully Aristotelian. The first is the idea that the writer should always include propaganda for his philosophy.

Under censorship, writers have always been ingenious about smuggling in propaganda between the lines, so that the authorities miss it. That is appropriate in a dictatorship (though somewhat foolish), but it is wrong in your own articles, particularly if you are an Objectivist. And certainly, when you write for a magazine whose philosophy you share, there is *no* reason to smuggle in your philosophy or preach it.

For example, someone submitted to *The Objectivist* a movie review that was chaos. I could not tell whether the author was reviewing a movie or preaching Objectivist morality. The two aspects were totally unintegrated. He would say something about the movie, and then start into a diatribe on the evil of presenting such immoral people. (It was a gangster movie.) The diatribe was not integrated with what he was saying about the movie. The author thought you could not review a movie of that sort without making it a platform for Objectivism. Of course, it was unconvincing in regard to the Objectivist slogans he used, and it was unconvincing as a review. He had two intentions: to say what he wanted about the movie, and to fulfill his "duty" to Objectivism. Well, that was the attitude at the height of the Middle Ages, when nothing was permitted except what led to the greater glory of the Church.

Let the Objectivism in your article come naturally out of your material and your presentation of it. Never make the communication of your philosophy a special assignment—that belongs in theoretical articles only. When you write on philosophical theory, you *are* preaching Objectivism in the sense that you are demonstrating a new aspect of the philosophy. But in a middle-range article, do not attempt to sell or prove Objectivism. Do not "stick in" your philosophy. Simply use it as your implicit framework. If, for example, an Objectivist were writing on modern art, he would not tell you why reason is good and irrationality bad, nor would he prove that reason is man's means of survival. His condemnation of modern art would be based on the fact that he expects reason in the arts. For the purpose of the article, he would take this as an axiom, though it certainly is not; it would take a long development to prove that reason is important. But the article, in presenting the irrationality of modern art, would imply in every line that irrationality is evil and ridiculous, and that reason is important and good. The author would apply those aspects of Objectivism that are relevant to art. Such an article is not a propaganda piece. It is written from a philosophical frame of reference which gives it unity and coherence. But its purpose is only to tell you the state of modern art.

In preparation for this topic, I went over some of my articles to find an example of not bringing in Objectivism. I did not find one: I propagandize for Objectivism constantly, in various degrees. But I bring it in, not by proving it, but by tying a given subject to its wider implications. That is because I am a theoretician—and it is something you should not yet emulate. After you have written many articles, it is all right to try tricky integrations; but not until then, because you would get lost in the theme and the side implications.

For example, in my "Brief Comment" on Apollo 8, I could have confined the article to the impropriety of reading the Bible from the spaceship. But I chose to bring in, at the end, a broader cultural issue, i.e., the breach between science and ethics. I knew how to do it, and the article remained integrated. But I could not have done it twenty years ago. Only after finishing *Atlas Shrugged* did I feel so at home in abstract issues that I could do tricky integrations without confusing the reader. So do not attempt it until you have enough experience.

It is not the duty of an Objectivist writer to smuggle in something to the glory of Objectivism, along the lines of waving the flag or a cross. When you write an article in which you evaluate cultural phenomena rationally, you do more for Objectivism than you could in any other form—even if you never mention reason, man, his means of survival, or any other Objectivist bromides which ritualistic "Objectivists" too often use inappropriately.

The second error sometimes committed by those who are not

fully Aristotelian is to believe that writing will somehow reveal evils in the writer's own subconscious. But this is not so. If, for example, you are an advocate of individualism, and you suddenly observe that you write like a collectivist, that is all right. That has taught you something; you have material you can correct. But to sit in fear, thinking: "I believe in Objectivism with all my soul, but what if the printed page shows me to be a monster?"—is to take a mystical approach, which indicates that you do not understand free will. There is nothing wrong in having "demons." What is wrong is evading them and doing nothing about them.

Some people think that when they write, they must practice Objectivist "company manners." Such a person guards his subconscious, because he worries that if he let himself go he might write improperly. *Nothing could be better calculated to stop you from writing.* In fact, the exact opposite premise is necessary. When you write, you must trust *your* subconscious, and more: you must allow your subconscious to be the sole authority in the universe. Otherwise you cannot write. This does not mean that man is only the subconscious and that the conscious mind does not count. It is the mind that uses the subconscious. But your subconscious is a programmed computer, and if it is programmed incorrectly, there is no way for you to write if you repress your machine.

In fact, if you *have* written some bad sentences, or expressed some wrong ideas, the conclusion should be *not* that your subconscious has demons, but that you did not think through the subject carefully and that your subconscious is fallible. But you are there to correct the mistake. Again, there is nothing wrong in making mistakes. What is wrong is not correcting them.

For a practical illustration and a good exercise, here is an article by James Reston on the present college situation. Try to identify the author's philosophy and the means by which you know it. You will thereby see how *he* introduces his philosophy (which is not mine) without preaching it. His method is, for the most part, correct.

"The Politics of Fear and Hope" by James Reston, The New York Times, May 6, 1969

The campus war never seemed more alarming than it does now, but it may be deceptive. It has gone so far and raised so many fears on all sides that, like the Vietnam war, it may have reached its peak and started the process of reappraisal and accommodation.

The experiment with coercion and physical force has been a disappointment to almost everybody who has tried it. The blacks used it at Cornell and made some progress at the start, but are still in deep trouble. The S.D.S. and the administration at Harvard tried to solve their differences by force and it was a stand-off. The resort to violence by both blacks and whites at City College in New York produced a bloody battle and startled everybody with the prospect of a racial massacre. And while the crisis continues, at least many of the leaders on all sides are beginning to wonder.

This includes the President [Nixon], the Attorney General and the more thoughtful legislators, faculty members and student leaders. They have all gone through a new experience. They have all now seen the dangers of confrontation politics, and most of them now seem to be calling for a pause and reconsideration of the current violent trend.

The presidents of Harvard and Cornell, for example, have been off-campus this week trying to deal with the public reaction to their recent crisis. Nathan Pusey of Harvard has been in Washington pleading with the Congress to give the universities another chance to deal with their problems without political interference. President James Perkins of Cornell has been in New York arguing for patience so that he and his faculty and students can try to find new ways of settling their differences, and both think that they now have a good chance, not for a solution, but for a livable compromise.

The case for giving them more time to work out their difficulties without political interference or punitive laws is strong. The university presidents, faculty members and students have learned a lot about themselves and their problems and need time for reflection.

The Cornell situation illustrates the point. The power of disciplining students there rested with the faculty, but in the public mind the responsibility for discipline lay with President Perkins, and this created a fundamental problem.

No matter what the Negro students did at Cornell, neither the faculty nor the students could agree to expel the black militants or their militant white allies, for this would mean not only making the rebels vulnerable to legal penalties, but leaving them vulnerable to the draft and service in Vietnam.

This is what has confused the issue of authority on many campuses. Moderate students, faculty members and administrators clearly do not approve the violent tactics of the white and black militants, but when condemning them and expelling them raises the question of drafting them into a war in Vietnam they oppose, they simply cannot do it.

What the crisis of the last few weeks has done, paradoxically, is to make all the adversaries in the struggle feel trapped in a wholly new and alarming situation which threatens them all. Most students have never been involved in such problems before. A great many faculty members, though they were responsible for student discipline, had never attended a single meeting on such problems or even heard a Negro speak on the issues. But now they have been compelled to put their minds to the problem for the first time. In this sense, the crisis of the last few weeks has been important, and university administrators, faculty and students are just now beginning to think seriously about how to get out of the thicket.

In short, Pusey of Harvard and Perkins of Cornell—to mention only two symbols—are beginning to think about their problems in a different way. Both are obviously in deep trouble. Both are confessing that they should have anticipated their problems better than they did; both have clearly been changed by the struggles of recent days, and both are asking for time.

It is a fair request. Every adversity has its uses and everybody has been through the fire at Harvard, Cornell and City College in the last month, and has begun to think of the consequences of violence for everybody. The militant Negro and S.D.S. students, of course, disagree; they have argued that violence is the answer, but even they are beginning to question and doubt. The crisis, as usual, has produced not only danger but opportunity, and if the reaction of Pusey and Perkins is any guide, we may be turning back toward common sense.

What is Reston's philosophy, and how do we know that?

Reston believes there are no absolutes. In fact, he does not raise the issue of right and wrong at all. For example, he treats force as merely one method men can resort to. He is neither for nor against violence; he is neutral about it—and everything else. This is strong evidence that his philosophy is *pragmatism*. He does not pass judgment on either side—he simply says force does not work, and therefore we should return to common sense. The words "common sense" are the mystical talisman of the pragmatist.

According to pragmatism, principles cannot be discovered in advance. The only "principle" is that human beings have to act. But anything is permissible, because we cannot know in advance what is right. So Reston would never say, as an absolute, "Force is wrong and respect for individual rights is right." He would say, "If force does not work, one should not use it. If rights create a peaceful, prosperous society, then we should protect them—*if that is what we want.*" That is pragmatism.

Reston says the request for time is fair—that until they came to actual violence, neither the students, nor the faculty members, nor the administrators could know what to do. He does not ask why the administrators needed bloodshed and destruction before they realized they had to face the problem. He says simply that after this experience they are different and will think in a different way. That is pure pragmatism. (As Leonard Peikoff pointed out to me, this is straight from the pragmatist philosopher John Dewey, who held that thinking is a "disease." On Dewey's view, a person does not have to think unless he has a problem; it is normal and proper not to think, but to function habitually. But when something happens unexpectedly, which he cannot react to normally, he lacks ease. Thus, thinking is a *disease* caused by a new situation, in which one's habitual reactions do not "work.")

The reliance on emotions as a primary is another sign that Reston's philosophy is pragmatism. He says most students, faculty members, and administrators do not approve of violence; but when it comes to the government drafting the violent demonstrators into war, the students et al. simply cannot allow it. This is not an issue of right or wrong—of principles. Rather, he believes that if they *feel* they cannot send men to be drafted, that is an irreducible primary to which they must adjust.

Note that all of these points are good examples of how, properly, to introduce an idea as an axiom. Reston never questions the idea that a person cannot know in advance the consequences of his actions—that one must first act, then observe the consequences, and then think. That is *his* absolute. When you read his article, you know what he is saying, though he never states it explicitly. That is the proper way to present a philosophy, without propagandizing, in a middle-range article.

Nevertheless, Reston's article is somewhat dishonest (this is inherent in pragmatism) in that he does not state explicitly the conclusion implied throughout his article, and which he names only once, indirectly: "a livable compromise." My own conclusion would be that the students' initiation of force is the major evil, which has primacy over every other consideration. I can say that openly. But as a pragmatist, Reston cannot say openly what he implies, namely, that the solution to every problem is compromise. If he said that, as a firm absolute, he would be contradicting pragmatism, which claims there are no absolutes. Furthermore, he and everyone else would see that what he is advocating is immoral.

If you want to know how a pragmatist would properly propagandize, read the works of William James and John Dewey. They wrote theoretical works devoted to proving that you cannot know anything, that abstract principles are not valid, and that we must judge solely according to what "works." To propagandize *im*properly, in a middle-range article, a dogmatic pragmatist would out of nowhere bring in theory and start preaching that you cannot know anything. He would explicitly say that since neither the activists nor the administrators can know anything in advance, they could not have avoided their situation, and so should be given more time.

Reston's article, though, is not propaganda. He is a commentator, writing about current events and merely suggesting a certain viewpoint. Yet notice all that we were able to conclude about his philosophy. So if you wrote a similar article from an Objectivist viewpoint, you would not have to announce: "Because such and such is man's nature, we must respect individual rights, which can be violated only by force; therefore I am against force." If you tried to squeeze all of that in, your article would be very ineffective. In a sense, Reston is preaching pragmatism more effectively than James and Dewey—though he could not have done it without them—because the average person reading James and Dewey takes them to mean only that you ought to be practical; he never grasps what pragmatism really preaches.

Now, how would I write on this issue, applying my philosophy properly? In what follows, I do not rewrite the article; I present only a sketch of what I would write if I accepted the same structure and facts as Reston, but not the same interpretation of those facts.

In the first paragraph, Reston says that the situation on campus is alarming, but that there may be hope. I would start by saying the situation is more alarming than ever, because the universities are now giving in to physical force. Then I would discuss Cornell, Harvard, and CCNY. But instead of saying there was disappointment on both sides, though some progress was made at Cornell, I would say that at Cornell the activists used force—including guns on campus—and have so far achieved their objective. I would say that at Harvard they used force, and the faculty gave in (on Black Studies and other demands); and, when the university made an attempt at self-defense by calling the police, the moderate students—the majority—suddenly supported the activists. I would then comment that the moderates did not mind the *initiation* of force, only the retaliation against it. Next I would mention that at CCNY, the violence approached racial warfare, which is significant because the student demands were made in the name of antiracism, and yet led to racial violence. Then I would say that the President, Attorney General, legislators, faculty members, and student leaders seem to object, but it is interesting that they do not know what to do.

At this point I would say Pusey and Perkins, who are both in trouble, are asking for more time. I would point out that they had warnings, and that as the presidents of major universities they should have had some kind of program worked out. Why do they believe that if they could not solve their problems so far, time will help them? Nothing new has happened. Therefore, their behavior indicates that their main purpose is to pretend that the situation is not as bad as it is. They are afraid of the situation, and of political interference or "repression." So they take no sides, not even the side of self-protection. (If the police offered them protection, they would not accept it.) They would rather go on as they were, pretending they had authority and pretending they were negotiating something. But they do not know what to negotiate, and have no means of arriving at the answer.

Then I would bring in Vietnam. Some of the reluctance on the part of the moderates is due to their opposition to the war in Vietnam, and thus they sympathize with the dissenters, who, if expelled, would be drafted. I would reply that quite apart from whether the draft is moral—and it is not—the real questions are: Does such sympathy justify the use of violence by the students? Shouldn't the objection to force be placed above sympathy for victims of the draft law? Which is more important?

Next I would say that everyone involved feels trapped—except for the activists, who are getting what they want. Why do all the others feel trapped? Here I can observe what Reston does, but apply it in a different context. They feel trapped because they have no principles to tell them how to get out of this situation. They are being attacked by force, yet they have no knowledge of the appropriate means of dealing with force. They do not know what is right or wrong. They never had to think about this before because the issue never came up, but now reality is forcing them to think. Then I would ask: Does reality force men to think? If Pusey and Perkins feel they are changed, what changed them? Obviously, nothing new has come up. They say that now they will act differently—they are beginning to think of the consequences. But by what means will they judge these?

At this point I would come out in the open: Since we know their philosophy is pragmatism, it is clear that pragmatism does not work. What they need are principles. And I would add that in social issues, the first such principle is the noninitiation of force.

Observe that I do not bring in Objectivist propaganda, I merely raise certain questions and evaluate certain events. Only at the end, when the events have demonstrated it, do I say pragmatism does not work.

If you did write about the same subject in the way Reston does, i.e., evaluating the events, ascribing motives, and prescribing policies, it would be a strong article. And it *would* sell Objectivism, but only by indirection—which is all a middle-range article should do. Just give your audience the facts from the Objectivist viewpoint, and let their minds do the rest. A rational reader who has never heard of Objectivism will think: "Yes, force should not be used. In fact, no social issue is more important than that. If you resort to force, there can be no discussion, no rights, no principles." If he draws only that conclusion, his mind will do the rest if he is mentally active. You have given him a lead to further thinking.

To sum up: the purpose of a middle-range article is to evaluate a given concrete from the point of view of your philosophy—i.e., holding your philosophy as a frame of reference and taking it as a given—but not to preach it or prove that it is right. Never try to prove your philosophy as a side issue in an article dealing with some narrow subject. If you feel that there is some aspect of your philosophy which requires proof, then write a theoretical article on it.

5

Creating an Outline

No beginner should write without an outline. If I could enforce this as an absolute, I would. Most writing problems—the psychological barriers, setbacks, discouragements—come from the absence of a proper outline. One reason for the dreadful articles in our media is that they are written without outlines, and thus fall apart structurally.

Good articles (regardless of whether you agree with them) are done from written outlines. Experienced professionals can work from mental outlines (if the article is brief enough), but that is a stage few writers ever reach, and beginners should not try it. If you do, you will only discourage yourself and end up wondering why you cannot write.

If you properly delimit your subject and theme, you have the base for your outline.

An outline is a plan of mental action. All human action requires a plan—an abstract projection. People tend to be aware of this in the physical realm. But because they believe that writing is an innate talent, they think it does not require an objective plan. They think writing is inspirational. Yet trying to write without an outline is even more difficult than attempting some physical action without a plan.

You would be surprised how often you make the equivalent of an outline in your mind for daily activities. You select a goal and the key steps that will take you there, and then you determine the details for each step.

For example, assume you have decided to make a dress and have determined what kind of dress it will be. That is the equivalent of selecting your subject and theme. You then take the measurements and devise a pattern, which is your outline. Then you cut the material, you sew it, and, finally, you embroider it. Now suppose a beginner started cutting and embroidering at the same time, without having chosen the type of dress or the material to be used. He would surely get into trouble. In principle, the process is exactly the same for writing (and for any other job).

The basic pattern of an outline is that of a theorem of Euclidean geometry: state what you are going to demonstrate, demonstrate it, and then announce the conclusion. An outline, however, involves more steps and details. Also, since this basic pattern does not yet tell you how to organize the concretes of your particular subject, there are many options. (For example, you do not *have* to start an article by announcing, "I am going to prove that . . .") But broadly speaking, you should, in your outline, state your subject, set up the logical progression of arguments, and in conclusion state the climax.

In the beginning of an article, but not necessarily in the first paragraph, you must let the reader know what your article is about. (You could call this the introduction.) You need not explicitly name what you are going to prove, because that would produce an anticlimax. But let the reader know where you are taking him. Incidentally, by "introduction," I mean introductory remarks—a good opening paragraph or so in which you indicate what your subject is. Do not make a special production of this. Introductions as such really pertain to books [see chapter 9]. As a rule, you do not need to write a formal introduction to an article, as some writing courses claim. That is completely artificial.

The "climax" in a nonfiction article is the point at which you demonstrate what you set out to demonstrate. It might require a single paragraph or several pages. There are no rules here. But in preparing the outline, you must keep in mind where you start from (i.e., your subject) and where you want to go (i.e., your theme—the conclusion you want your reader to reach). These two terminal points determine how you will get from one to the other. In good fiction, the climax—which you must know in advance—determines what events you need in order to bring the story to that point. In nonfiction too, your conclusion gives you a lead to the steps needed to bring the reader to the climax.

The guiding question in this process is: What does the reader need to know in order to agree with the conclusion? That determines what to include. Select the essentials of what you need in order to convince the reader—keeping in mind the context of your subject. You are not starting from a *tabula rasa*. If you were, your reader would not know how to read English, but you could not teach him that while writing on a more advanced subject. When you ask yourself what the reader needs to know, you ask it only in regard to your specific subject, not in regard to his general knowledge.

You must also keep in mind the scale of your article. This might be difficult at first, but with experience it becomes easier to project *how much* you can cover. In the beginning, the tendency is to try to cover too much. For example, as you begin to write from your outline, you may find that you have used over half the space intended for your article on just the first of ten points. This happens to every writer who attempts ambitious themes, because there is always something to add. You discover that you actually have three articles contained in your outline, instead of one. But with a few properly written articles (i.e., written from a proper outline), the process of gauging the size of your work becomes almost automatic.

I do not mean you can judge, to the last page, the length of your article. But you must have some idea as to whether you are writing a one-page article, a six-page article, or an indeterminate volume. You have to adjust the projection of your theme to a certain size— for example, no smaller than five pages and no bigger than eight. These are not absolute figures, but an approximation. So set yourself a minimum length you can do it in and a maximum over which you must not go. This gives you a standard for judging how detailed to make your article, what points are essential, and what points are dispensable subcategories or sidelines.

It is crucial to state your theme properly to yourself. For example, the theme of "The 'Inexplicable Personal Alchemy' " is: the horrible destruction of the best among the young people in Russia and in America, and the comparison between the two. Stated that way, it entails too many things. My next step was to decide what the key points of the subject are which convey this theme. I then listed all such points, then selected the essential ones and omitted the others. This determined what I would have to say to demonstrate my theme.

The theme is the standard by which you judge whether to include or omit some point. Suppose you are tempted to include an interesting sideline. Ask yourself whether the point is necessary to demonstrate your theme. And conversely, before omitting something, ask yourself whether your case will be fully demonstrated if you omit this point. This is all part of the process of deciding on your outline—deciding what is needed to demonstrate your theme.

The logical order of presentation is also determined by the theme. After you decide on your theme and write down the steps that will convince your reader of it, you will see that there are some options about which steps should precede which. (This is still in the pre-outline stage.) But to discover the overall logical continuity, look for causal connections among the steps of your argument. If you retrace what you had to know to arrive at a conclusion, and then what the reader needs to know to arrive at it, you will see that *some* of the steps are the logical consequences of earlier ones. The nearest to a rule of logical continuity is: observe the law of causality—i.e., observe which of your points depend on which.

There are no rules about how long or detailed an outline should be. It depends on each individual: *you* must judge how detailed a plan of action you need for what you have undertaken.

The outline's level of detail depends on how clear the subject is in your mind, and how complex the article is. I suggest the following test. If in making an outline you feel vaguely that some point is difficult to formulate, though you "kind of" know what you mean, then you need more detail. On the other hand, if you begin to feel bored—if all you need are a few lines on some point but you are writing a volume—then you are being too detailed. As in all mental activity, you are the only judge.

It may help to work in layers. First make a brief outline, then, before you start writing, elaborate on certain points and make something between a first draft and a bare outline. Be honest with yourself. Decide how much of a general map you need to make the content of your article fully clear to you, in essentials and in an orderly form, before you start writing. When in doubt, remember the purpose of the outline. It is *your* blueprint. Only you can tell to what extent you should expand it and what you can leave to logical implication.

Some people think an outline should be so detailed that it is almost as long as the future article. Nothing could be worse. That is not an outline, but a first draft. A first draft is a long, detailed piece in which you omit the polishing of your sentences and the fancier elaborations; but it is not an outline. If that is what you have written, you have skipped the outline stage. It is easier—except in the consequences—to sit down and write a long outline; it is much harder to make a properly organized and condensed one.

I do not mean that you must write your outline in "headline" style (i.e., without complete sentences). That style is more appropriate to an experienced writer or to someone very familiar with his subject. But it can be deceptive. You may think you have clearly stated what you intend to write, and then find yourself departing from your outline because it was not precise enough. On the other hand, making an overly detailed outline is as bad as writing without one. So I urge beginners to write a brief outline, but in grammatical sentences.

When you make an outline, do not write: "Introduction. Progression. Conclusion." That is far too abstract and thus useless. You need something many levels less abstract than that. Say you are writing an article critical of the Nixon administration. If you put in your outline: "Introduction of my subject," that is too broad. Instead write, as Point 1: "Introduction—express general reasons why I am dissatisfied and puzzled by Nixon's behavior so far." That is a very generalized statement, which you could not use in an article, but it is specific enough for your own guidance (and it is grammatical).

Then list, on a separate piece of paper, the main points you want to cover concerning your dissatisfaction. Assume you are dissatisfied with his stands on Vietnam, welfare, and taxes. Say you decide that the most crucial of these three—i.e., the worst—is his welfare policy. So you list it last, for dramatic progression. (If you list your most important objection first, you will produce an anticlimax.) Thus, you write under Point 2: "Nixon's tax policy: I shall indicate how this represents a broken campaign promise, and why it is dangerous to pursue the same tax policy as that of the Johnson administration." These are connected sentences, not headlines. They are just specific enough for you to know what to present fully in that part of the article.

Then under Point 3, write something like: "Nixon's Vietnam policy: Briefly cover the essence of what was wrong with the Johnson policy. Indicate in what way Nixon seems to be continuing the same policy. Mention what indication he has given that he has no new approach." This is abstract, but it will delimit what you say about his Vietnam policy. Finally, you come to the climax: his continuation of the welfare state. Write under Point 4: "Welfare: He is reshuffling the various agencies without eliminating the improper services. He is vacillating with his 'war on poverty' and his constant welfare-state promises." You might even include here: "I shall quote, for illustration, certain points." You proceed to list the facts that show his welfare policy to be dubious. Finally, you come to Point 5, your conclusion. Since it is a critical article, you draw some kind of conclusion in order not to leave your reader hanging. So you might write (if this is what you have proven): "Conclusion: I think we can give him more time; I am not yet sure that his administration will be bad, though I have serious doubts." Or: "I think he has indicated enough to make me conclude that nothing is to be expected of his administration. He is a variant of Johnson."

You should have your conclusion in mind from the start (though not necessarily verbatim). Know the point of your article, whether cautious optimism or wary doubts or total pessimism, before you decide to write. Then, as you make your outline, write down your conclusion as explicitly as you can (though not necessarily in detail), so that it is clear to you. That sets up a standing order in your mind, which helps in the actual process of writing. It serves as a reference point whenever you are in doubt during the writing, particularly about side issues or elaborations. It tells you whether a point you are about to include is necessary or not.

The conclusion—the theme—is your best criterion for composing the outline; make it *explicit*. Some of the greatest troubles here come from mental approximation, when you "sort of" know what you want to say. The fact is you do *not* know, in the full epistemological sense, until your thought is conceptualized in grammatical form. Until then, you have only the material which you can organize into knowledge. In this sense, an outline is also helpful in formalizing and, therefore, in firming up, your knowledge.

A proper outline is so dependent on the nature of your theme that it is impossible to make many absolute rules about it. A rule such as: "Give three paragraphs to your introduction, ten to the development, and one to the conclusion" is a kind of classicism (which I discuss and condemn in "What is Romanticism?"[1]). It is the substitution of concretes for abstractions, and it becomes an artificial straitjacket into which you are forced to fit your material. General principles can be stated and followed, but there are no rules for the application of these principles to the concretes of a given article.

What I have given you so far is positive advice. I next want to mention some common problems to be avoided in making an outline.

The Temptation to Include Sidelines

By "sidelines" I mean (1) issues which are connected to your subject and theme, but are not a necessary part of them, or (2) illustrations or applications from completely new areas. This danger is particularly great with middle-range articles. For example, you are discussing politics and you see brilliant sidelines in physics or psy-

---

[1] *The Romantic Manifesto*. She writes: "Classicism . . . was a [literary] school that had devised a set of arbitrary, *concretely* detailed rules purporting to represent the final and absolute criteria of esthetic value" (p. 104).

chology or esthetics, and want to squeeze them in. That can destroy your article.

The wider and more integrated your knowledge, the more you will be tempted to include sidelines. This temptation comes from a good psycho-epistemology, because you *should* make connections with everything you learn. Writing articles, however, is not learning, but communicating knowledge. For that, you must break up your integrations and judge, as you make your outline, which points are essential and which are merely interesting sidelines. If they are sidelines, omit them (especially if you are a beginner).

The Platonic Approach to Logical Order

There is a dangerous misconception about outlines, namely, that there is only *one* possible logical order of presentation.

In the sense in which an outline is like a geometric theorem, there *is* only one order. But when you write an article, you do not confine yourself to three large abstractions, like a syllogism: premise A, premise B, and the conclusion. An article does follow that broad pattern, but under each of these basic divisions there are many details from which you must choose. Only a very simple article with a very simple theme would have only one possible order of presentation. No worthwhile subject is so simple that there is only one logical order—*the* one order which would determine every paragraph.

Suppose the subject is politics. An author might think there is only one logical order which, if he knew it, would make him discuss elections first, taxes second, and the welfare state third. But then he starts to wonder: "Or is it in reverse? Or maybe the second point is first and the third point second?" Etc. Many people approach this with a Platonic outlook, which holds that there is only one "ideal" order; and too often they conclude that since they do not know what it is, they will write without *any* order.

The principles behind determining the order of an outline are abstractions subsuming a vast number of concretes. You can establish rules about these principles, but not about the use of concretes. No set of principles can give you the *one* logical order.

The Concrete-Bound Approach to Logical Order

Many people are concrete-bound in regard to their outline, and this approach affects the structure of their articles. Such writers see an article as a series of separate points. For example, Point 1 may lead logically to Point 2, but Point 2 has no relation to Point 3. Point 3 may be connected to Points 4 and 5, but one does not know why Point 6 is included. Consequently, logical connections might be made from paragraph to paragraph, or from one sequence to another, but the total is not well integrated. When you read the whole article, you are not sure what the author's theme is—i.e., the article does not seem to be centered on any particular issue.

This is an error not of knowledge or content, but of writing without a proper outline. While a writer should concentrate on the particular sentence or paragraph he is working on, the concrete-bound author has a totally nearsighted view. He loses sight of the article as a whole. He does not keep in mind the continuity of the total, i.e., the relationship between each sequence and all the others.

A well-integrated article requires an outline that is detailed enough to be clear, but not so detailed that it fails to isolate the essentials. The essentials are needed for you to retain that abstract integration during the entire writing process.

Mistaking Relevance for Logical Continuity

Some beginners write the outline as if they were throwing disconnected pieces of thought down on paper. For example, an author decides to write on capitalism. He has a wide context of relevant ideas, and begins to write almost inspirationally. His only sense of continuity is some loose relevance to capitalism. He thinks that somehow all the pieces will integrate into a coherent point. There is nothing wrong with mulling over a subject in this loose way—if you are *thinking* about it and not yet writing. But never take that process as the equivalent of an outline, because it is the opposite.

I would like to suggest the following exercise. I will present a brief article of mine. Your assignment is to make an outline of it in a form sufficient for you to write from. My purpose is to help you learn how to analyze or reconstruct something already written, so that you can then reverse the procedure and make an outline on your own. (Afterwards, I will provide the outline I used in writing it.)

In my outlines I use a headline style, rather than full grammatical sentences. After much experience, you can use a shorthand too and know its exact meaning. But at the beginning, in order to automatize the outline-article relationship, use full sentences.

As you read the following article, write down its *essentials*. This enables you to see the overall logical order of the presentation, and to avoid being confused about why one paragraph follows another.

Here is the article:

"Doesn't Life Require Compromise?"[2]

A compromise is an adjustment of conflicting claims by mutual concessions. This means that both parties to a compromise have some valid claim and some value to offer each other. And *this* means that both parties agree upon some fundamental principle which serves as a base for their deal.

It is only in regard to concretes or particulars, implementing a mutually accepted basic principle, that one may compromise. For instance, one may bargain with a buyer over the price one wants to receive for one's product, and agree on a sum somewhere between one's demand and his offer. The mutually accepted basic principle, in such case, is the principle of trade, namely: that the buyer must pay the seller for his product. But if one wanted to be paid and the alleged buyer wanted to obtain one's product for nothing, no compromise, agreement or discussion would be possible, only the total surrender of one or the other.

There can be no compromise between a property owner and a

[2]Ayn Rand, *The Virtue of Selfishness: A New Concept of Egoism* (New York: New American Library, 1964).

burglar; offering the burglar a single teaspoon of one's silverware would not be a compromise, but a total surrender—the recognition of his *right* to one's property. What value or concession did the burglar offer in return? And once the principle of unilateral concessions is accepted as the base of a relationship by both parties, it is only a matter of time before the burglar would seize the rest. As an example of this process, observe the present [1962] foreign policy of the United States.

There can be no compromise between freedom and government controls; to accept "just a few controls" is to surrender the principle of inalienable individual rights and to substitute for it the principle of government's unlimited, arbitrary power, thus delivering oneself into gradual enslavement. As an example of this process, observe the present domestic policy of the United States.

There can be no compromise on basic principles or on fundamental issues. What would you regard as a "compromise" between life and death? Or between truth and falsehood? Or between reason and irrationality?

Today, however, when people speak of "compromise," what they mean is not a legitimate mutual concession or a trade, but precisely the betrayal of one's principles—the unilateral surrender to any groundless, irrational claim. The root of that doctrine is *ethical subjectivism*, which holds that a *desire* or a *whim* is an irreducible moral primary, that every man is entitled to any desire he might feel like asserting, that all desires have equal moral validity, and that the only way men can get along together is by giving in to anything and "compromising" with anyone. It is not hard to see who would profit and who would lose by such a doctrine.

The immorality of this doctrine—and the reason why the term "compromise" implies, in today's general usage, an act of moral treason—lies in the fact that it requires men to accept ethical subjectivism as the basic principle superseding all principles in human relationships and to sacrifice anything as a concession to one another's whims.

The question "Doesn't life require compromise?" is usually asked by those who fail to differentiate between a basic principle and some concrete, specific wish. Accepting a lesser job than one had wanted is *not* a "compromise." Taking orders from one's employer on how to do the work for which one is hired, is *not* a "compromise." Failing to have a cake after one has eaten it, is *not* a "compromise."

Integrity does not consist of loyalty to one's subjective whims, but of loyalty to rational principles. A "compromise" (in the unprincipled sense of that word) is not a breach of one's comfort, but a breach of one's convictions. A "compromise" does not consist of doing something one dislikes, but of doing something one knows to be evil. Accompanying one's husband or wife to a concert, when one does not care for music, is *not* a "compromise"; surrendering to his or her irrational demands for social conformity, for pretended religious observance or for generosity toward boorish in-laws, *is*. Working for an employer who does not share one's ideas, is *not* a "compromise"; pretending to share his ideas, *is*. Accepting a publisher's suggestions to make changes in one's manuscript, when one sees the rational validity of his suggestions, is *not* a "compromise"; making such changes in order to please him or to please "the public," against one's own judgment and standards, *is*.

The excuse, given in all such cases, is that the "compromise" is only temporary and that one will reclaim one's integrity at some indeterminate future date. But one cannot correct a husband's or wife's irrationality by giving in to it and encouraging it to grow. One cannot achieve the victory of one's ideas by helping propagate their opposite. One cannot offer a literary masterpiece, "when one has become rich and famous," to a following one has acquired by writing trash. If one found it difficult to maintain one's loyalty to one's own convictions at the start, a succession of betrayals—which helped to augment the power of the evil one lacked the courage to fight—will not make it easier at a later date, but will make it virtually impossible.

There can be no compromise on moral principles. "In any compromise between food and poison, it is only death that can win. In any compromise between good and evil, it is only evil that can profit." (*Atlas Shrugged.*) The next time you are tempted to ask: "Doesn't life require compromise?" translate that question into its actual meaning: "Doesn't life require the surrender of that which is true and good to that which is false and evil?" The answer is that *that* precisely is

what life forbids—if one wishes to achieve anything but a stretch of
tortured years spent in progressive self-destruction.

Here is the outline I used in writing the article:

Subject: the moral meaning of compromise.

Theme: the evil of compromise.

1. Definition of compromise. Need of basic principle as ground
   for proper compromise.
2. Impropriety of compromise on basic principles.
3. Modern view: ethical subjectivism. All desires are equally
   valid.
4. Cause of confusion is failure to differentiate between abstract
   basic principles and concrete wishes. Examples of what does
   and does not represent compromise.
5. The metaphysical meaning of compromise on moral principles.

This is not the way a beginner should construct an outline, because it is not detailed enough. But it is easy to follow, and it is necessary for organizing the details. It will be easier on you if you first
establish such a broad outline, and then fill in the necessary details.
Otherwise, you could miss some of them or put them in the wrong
place.

Sometimes an author becomes too abstract because he has not
quite decided what details he will use to illustrate something, and so
he begins to assert the arbitrary. On the other hand, a writer can add
good details but in such a disordered way that they do not integrate
into one structure. The broad outline protects against both errors.

Here is how a beginner might expand the outline I used. He
could, for example, include the actual definition of "compromise" in
Point 1, as well as what underlies it. For instance:

1. Definition of compromise: an adjustment of conflicting claims
   by mutual concessions.
   a. Need of basic principle as ground for proper compromise.

b. Presuppositions of a valid compromise:
   i. Both sides have some valid claim and some value to offer.
   ii. Both parties agree on an underlying principle.
   iii. The subject of the compromise is a concrete, not a principle.

Or you could expand Point 5:

5. The metaphysical meaning of compromise on moral principles. The question "Doesn't life require compromise?" is the same as "Doesn't life require the surrender of good to evil?"—which is precisely what life forbids.

[Editor's note: The appendix contains more of Ayn Rand's outlines.]

I shall conclude my discussion of outlines with two methodological points.

The most important one is what I call the "crow epistemology."[3] The purpose of an outline is to present your future article in a form you can grasp *as a unified whole*. This is why I stress that each person should make his outline to suit his own purposes. The exact form of your outline will depend on the subject and theme, and on how detailed or how abstract *you* need the outline to be in order to hold it all in your mind. So first make it abstract enough so that you can hold the total in your mind, and then, before you start writing, expand it by adding the necessary details. This way, you grasp the

[3]This expression, coined by Ayn Rand, is based on an experiment (mentioned in *Introduction to Objectivist Epistemology*, 2nd ed., p. 62) which showed that there was a limit to what a crow could hold in conscious awareness at one time. This limitation applies, *mutatis mutandis*, to human beings. Ayn Rand writes: "Since consciousness is a specific faculty, it has a specific nature or identity and, therefore, its range is limited: it cannot perceive everything at once; since awareness, on all its levels, requires an active process, it cannot do everything at once. Whether the units with which one deals are percepts or concepts, the range of what man can hold in the focus of his conscious awareness at any given moment, is limited" (p. 63).

connections between the overall structure of your article and the more concrete outline from which you will write.

Never start an article without knowing whether your structure is clear, organized, and properly delimited. If the abstract structure is not clear in your mind, you cannot hold in mind the overall view of your article or decide what belongs in it, so problems will arise. For example, you will be tempted to go into sidelines—and the article will fall apart.

Whenever you have a mental outline that is too narrow and detailed, tell yourself: "This is my subject. This is my material. Now, what exactly am I going to do?" Step back and look at the total. To "step back" means to look at the next level of abstraction. In effect, you condense your material, by essentials, as you ask yourself: "What am I actually doing?" You step back and look more abstractly at the same content—as abstractly as necessary in order to hold the overall view in your mind. When you reach that stage, you are in control.

This is actually the pre-outline stage. You start from scratch with a certain subject and theme, and a lot of material which is not yet organized in your mind. You then make the abstract outline, followed by the more detailed one. If you cannot do it this way, make a detailed outline first and then abstract to the general one. When you have both outlines—an overall view and a detailed skeleton—you can start the actual writing.

The second methodological point is the Aristotelian concept of final causation. Among Aristotle's four causes, the two that play a constant role in our lives are final causation and efficient causation. The latter operates at the level of inanimate matter: a certain cause is enacted and it has certain effects. Final causation, however, pertains only to consciousness. (Aristotle believed it also applies to nature, but that is a different issue.)

By final causation, Aristotle meant that a purpose is set in advance, and then the steps required to achieve it are determined. *This* is the process of causation that operates in human consciousness. To do anything, you must know what you want to achieve. For instance, if you decide to drive to Chicago, the roads you select, the amount of gas, etc., will be determined by that goal. But to get there, you will have to start a process of efficient causation, which includes filling the gas tank, starting the car, steering, etc. You will be following the laws of inanimate matter. But the whole process will be a chain of actions you have selected in order to achieve a certain purpose, namely, to get to Chicago.

In no human activity is final causation more important than in creative work, particularly in writing. In order to have a good outline, and later a good article, you must initiate a process of final causation. When in doubt about your outline, that is the test. You set yourself a definite purpose—i.e., you name explicitly your subject and theme—and *that* determines what material to choose in order to end up with an article that satisfies your purpose. It is final causation that determines what to include both in your outline and in your article.

To sum up, what you need most to make a proper outline are: (1) the concept of an essence—and the ability to distinguish essentials from details; and (2) the concept of causality—and the ability to establish cause-and-effect relations in the presentation of an idea. With these as your most important guidelines, your outline will probably be good.

6

Writing the Draft: The Primacy of the Subconscious

Writing involves both your conscious mind and your subconscious. This is an important psycho-epistemological fact affecting every stage of writing. Without the use of your subconscious, you cannot write (or speak). While complete knowledge of the role of the subconscious does not yet exist, there are helpful principles.

In general, writing problems come from not knowing when to use your conscious mind and when to rely on your subconscious. Of course, we use both elements all the time: a conscious mind cannot function without the storage house of the subconscious, and nobody can write using his subconscious alone (unless he is sleepwalking). But the distinction is that when you prepare an outline and when you edit, you function predominantly by means of your conscious mind. Naturally, you draw on your subconscious knowledge of the subject and on any subconscious integrations that give you inspirational ideas—but your conscious mind directs the process. When it comes to actually writing the draft, however, your subconscious must be in the driver's seat. Your conscious mind ensures that you are in focus, know what you are writing about, and are driving in the right direction. But for the *execution* of your purpose, you rely on your subconscious.

You cannot write by a fully conscious process. By "fully conscious" I mean that you make decisions according to your fully focused awareness. If you tried, you could not write a single sentence. If you tried to select every word by conscious decision, it would take years, because you would have to study a thesaurus for each one. Moreover, by the time you selected a couple of words, you would have forgotten what you wanted to say.

As an experiment, make yourself self-conscious and try to tell someone what you did this morning. Focus on what you are saying—on whether you are selecting the right words, the proper sentence structure, etc. You will stutter helplessly and be unable to finish a sentence. The same happens if you write by such overfocused, overconscious means. To speak or write, you must rely on your subconscious, automatized integrations.

When we speak, it feels as if the words come automatically—as if the words and thoughts come simultaneously. Of course, they do not. If you observe children learning to speak, or yourself learning a foreign language, you discover that language is not innate and automatic, but an acquired skill. It is so well integrated at the adult level, however, that the transition from the thought you want to express to the words you use to express it is automatic.

In writing, you need to establish the same kind of connection between your subconscious and the words you put on paper. Since any subject involves many complexities, the connection will never be quite so automatic or perfect. That is why editing is required. But while you are writing, do not act as an editor at the same time. Do not be self-conscious while writing. When you begin to write your first draft, let the words come automatically. Do not think over your sentences in advance and do not censor yourself.

If you want your overall style to be natural and consistent, do not be artificially stylized in the process of writing. Write directly from your subconscious, as the words come to you. Your writing might be primitive or even ungrammatical, but that can be corrected later.

Your outline sets the direction, and thus the standing orders, for your subconscious. You know your subject and what you want to say about it. But when it comes to *how* you are going to say it, you must trust your subconscious *as it is*.

It is a contradiction to think you can do better than your own mind, yet that is what the overcritical approach amounts to. No matter what the state of your subconscious—whether or not you have the requisite writing skill and knowledge of the subject—it is your only tool. So do not demand the impossible of yourself. Do not set a preconceived standard of what to expect from your subconscious. You can apply editorial principles consciously, later; but if you do it in the process of writing, it will be torture and you will achieve nothing. When you edit, you can conclude that your subconscious was not functioning well, and even arrive at principles for self-improvement. But while you are writing, you must adopt the premise: my subconscious, right or wrong. You must let your automatic connections function, because you have no others.

The subconscious is not an entity with a mind of its own. It is like a computer and will do what you consciously order it, within the limits of its knowledge and training. In the process of writing, you will discover (if you introspect well) how sensitive your subconscious is and how careful you must be in using it. For instance, your subconscious will reflect exactly what *your* greatest concern is. If you focus on whether people will like your article, what it will do to your self-esteem, whether it is beautiful, etc., you will not squeeze out a sentence an hour, and will wonder why your thoughts do not flow freely. The reason is that your subconscious is obeying you. If you are concerned with an estimate ahead of the facts, it will obey and will not be interested in writing. It will be busy with self-esteem problems (e.g., whether your writing reveals talent) or editorial problems (e.g., whether you write beautifully). As a result, you will be paralyzed.

When you write, be as conceited as you can be—"conceit" is not the right word, but I want to overstate the point. You must have total self-esteem. Leave your self-doubts behind when you sit down to write—and pick them up again, if you wish, during the process of editing. Sometimes your writing will give you reason to feel some self-doubt afterward (but this should be temporary, if you are disappointed in what you read the next day). But while you are writing, you must be God's perfect creature (if there were a God). Regard yourself as an absolute, sovereign consciousness. Forget that man is fallible and that you might make mistakes. That is true, but it is for the next day, when you edit.

Trust your subconscious by writing as if everything that comes out of it is right. This is an advance vote of self-confidence. It is not self-delusion, because it is true in this respect: the freer your mind, the more clearly you will see its exact capacity and knowledge on a given issue. If you rely on your subconscious without repression or self-doubt, you will discover the best your subconscious can do. For the purpose of *your* writing, in fact, there is nothing other than the process of your own creative subconscious, and you must trust it. You cannot do any better spontaneously. You *can* do better when you edit, but when writing, keep going without looking back.

Your conscious mind while writing should be concerned with your subject. You must focus, with full confidence in your ability to say something important, on the subject and theme—and let your subconscious provide the words to express exactly what you want to say. The decisions concerning what you want to say and in what order have been made beforehand, in your outline—and any doubts you have should be reserved for the outline. But since an outline is very abstract, you cannot know in advance *exactly* what you will say. That comes only during the process of writing. To perform that process effectively, make your subject clear to yourself as you write— as clear as possible without pausing on every sentence.

This is what it means to trust your subconscious. Give your subconscious the standing order that you are concerned only with your subject and the clearest presentation of it possible, and let that be the absolute directing your writing. If something bothers you on the periphery of your consciousness—some distraction or self-doubt— ignore it; if it is serious, stop writing. But do not attempt to write with half your mind on the subject and the other half on irrelevant problems.

The simplest sentence requires your subconscious connections— and thus a clear knowledge of the subject. To write even a short article, you must know much more than you put on paper. For a book, you must know the equivalent of ten books, so that you can exercise selectivity and be sure about what you say. But if you tell your subconscious: "I sort of know my subject, and while writing I'll figure out what's unclear when I come to it," you will never come to it. Your subconscious will stop, because it will not know what to tell you.

Someone asked me the following question: Should you have all your ideas thought out before you begin the first draft, or can you learn as you are writing? And my answer is that you can sometimes do the second accidentally—but God help you if you attempt to do it deliberately. *Do not try to do your thinking and your writing at the same time.* A clear outline helps you avoid this problem. While you are writing, it allows you to focus your attention exclusively on conveying your thoughts in an objective, grammatical form.

These are two separate jobs: the job of thinking and the job of expressing your thoughts. And they cannot be done together. If you try, it will take you much longer, and be much more painful, than if you did each one separately—because you are giving your subconscious contradictory orders. You are saying: "I have to express something—but I do not know what."

It is true that you might start writing with a full understanding of your subject, and some new aspect suddenly occurs to you. You might put down a certain formulation, which then raises a question you never faced before. That is a normal process. And it would be perfectly appropriate to stop writing and think this question over. Or you might even inspirationally get the answer right away. But never *start* with a question mark in your mind.

In the process of writing, it is crucial not to stop for too long (and preferably not at all). For instance, if you have two hours assigned to writing, write during that time without stopping. (No one besides a hack can write for much more than two hours straight, except when there is unusual inspiration at the end of a work.) If you can write continuously, chances are that your work will require the least editing. But if you pause after every sentence to reread and rewrite it, you will have a lot of trouble in editing. One of the deadliest obstacles to good writing is critical overconscientiousness exercised *during* the process of writing.

If, as you write something, a better way of saying it spontaneously occurs to you, make the change. That is still a subconscious process: your subconscious gave you preliminary data and then fed you more refined data. But if the change requires a switch to a conscious state, do not do it.

I find the best way to write is not sentence by sentence (more on that error shortly), but sequence by sequence. By "sequence" I mean a subdivision of your outline. Since an outline is broken up into sequences, each point of an outline stands for a certain progression of thought. The best way to write is by such sequences, unless a given point is too lengthy.

Take a look at your outline before you start, and then do not stop yourself—do not edit, and do not look at your outline—until you finish that sequence. For example, suppose the first sequence of your outline, Point 1, is called "Presentation of the General Subject," and you know what you want to say. Start writing and do not stop until you are ready for Point 2. Then you can look at your outline and see what the second sequence is, etc.

This suggestion is not an absolute. If you find yourself confused or stymied—for example, because you went off on a sideline—then you may need to stop and check your outline. But short of such necessity, for rapid and well-integrated writing do not look at your outline too closely. Train yourself to write from an abstraction. If you constantly consult the same point in your outline, you will find your words stilted; after repeating the generalized sentence from your outline, you will have nothing more to say. The reason is that you have given your subconscious the order to say only what you wrote in your outline.

Your outline sets the direction. Keep that direction firmly in mind, but leave yourself free to express each point fully.

I cannot literally teach you to write. I can provide only a set of shortcuts that are helpful as general principles. These shortcuts will save you from bewilderment and from having to discover them slowly by yourself. To this end, there are a few errors or problems I want to warn you against, all involving the role of the subconscious in writing.

The Squirms

The "squirms" is a term coined by my husband, Frank, for a state of writing which is universal. It describes the following situation: you are writing, and suddenly, on a given sequence or chapter, you find yourself completely paralyzed mentally. This strikes at unexpected moments.

In writing *Atlas Shrugged*, for example, there were difficult sequences, and I was prepared for trouble; but when I got to them they almost wrote themselves. Then there were sequences which I thought were perfectly clear in my mind, but when I got to *them*, I found myself stopped for days. I could neither write nor give up the attempt.

My husband called this the squirms simply by watching my behavior. I usually do not discuss my writing troubles during such periods. But Frank can tell, because it *is* an inner agony. It is probably the worst experience, psychologically, that I know of. But when you solve the squirms, it loses all reality and the final result is worth the effort. That is the only consolation I can give you for one of the worst penalties of writing.

I asked many writers about this problem, and they all experienced it, with the exception of two Hollywood hacks who worked from 9 to 1, produced the same number of pages every day, and never had any trouble. Of course, this lack of squirms showed in their work. But writers of ability all go through the process.

There is a good book by Eliot Hutchinson entitled *How to Think Creatively*,[1] in which he discusses the squirms in great detail. He has his own terminology—for example, he calls the point at which this inner conflict ends "the moment of insight"—but it is the same process no matter what you call it. He has some good descriptions of it and some proper advice to give.

Let me describe what the squirms feel like. You find, suddenly, that your subconscious does not function. You know, consciously, what you want to say, but somehow the words do not come. One sign that you are in this state is that suddenly you write like a high school

[1]New York: Abingdon-Cokesbury Press, 1959.

student. Everything comes out in that flat, "the-cat-is-on-the-mat" style, like a dry summary, wooden and artificial. Yet your writing lacks even the virtue of clarity. I do not try to write more than two sentences in that state. If you force yourself, you will have spent a day in agony, only to discover the next morning that you can use nothing of what you wrote.

The squirms make you feel ignorant about writing. During such periods, I literally felt that it was impossible to write. I told myself consciously that I had written before; but emotionally, in that moment, I felt I had lost the very concept of writing. Simultaneously, you feel as if the solution is right there, and that if you tried harder you would break through. It almost makes you feel guilty, because it feels as if there is *something* you could do if you really wanted to— and you want to desperately, but can do nothing.

Most of *Atlas Shrugged* was written that way. I had worse squirms on that book than on anything I ever wrote, even though I knew much more about writing than I did when I wrote *The Fountainhead* or *We the Living*. In writing *Atlas*, I discarded five pages for every one that I kept, and it was torture. There were certainly inspirational passages—passages that wrote themselves—but only as a rare reward.

If you write something at all complex, you will experience the squirms in one form or another. The main reason for it is a subconscious contradiction. On the conscious level, in my case, I would create an outline, and my subject and theme would be perfectly clear to me. Only there were so many possibilities of which I was not aware—so many different ways of executing the theme—that my conscious mind in fact had *not* chosen clearly. Because of the complexity of the theme, I could not select clearly, in advance, from the many possibilities; hence, there were problems for my subconscious.

I had terrible squirms in writing *Atlas* because of the complexity of the integrations in that novel. I had to proceed slowly, because there was much more to integrate than in *The Fountainhead*, for instance. If you compare the two novels, especially their themes and sentence structures (i.e., what those sentences have to carry), you will observe that in *Atlas* I had to do much more. It was a process of constant writing, polishing, and rewriting, until I got all of those intentions into one scene or one page.

Another reason was that the background of *Atlas* was not familiar to me. Although I had done sufficient research, there was a strain in projecting how a scientist would feel, how Dagny Taggart would feel running a railroad, etc. After all, I was not writing naturalistically from my own experience. Now I had had to do the same kind of research for *The Fountainhead*, since architecture is not my profession, but that was only one profession. In *Atlas*, I wrote from the perspective of many different professions, none of them my own (except Hugh Akston's, in part, and he is a minor character).

Whenever you experience the squirms, some clash of intentions occurs on the subconscious level, as if your inner circuits were tied in knots. You feel paralyzed because your subconscious is struggling with a contradiction, but since it is on the subconscious level, you cannot identify it immediately.

On projects simpler than a novel, the problem could be a contradiction in what you want to say about your subject. Suppose there are two closely related aspects of your subject. Subconsciously you may vacillate between these aspects, thereby short-circuiting your subconscious. It is a problem of uncertainty. Although you think you made a clear decision about what to say, when it comes to elaborating it on paper you are uncertain, and this paralyzes your subconscious.

Another possible source of the squirms is a lack of knowledge. For example, on a given passage, you find you have insufficient knowledge to deal with a particular aspect of your subject. This stops you suddenly; you need an example, say, and cannot come up with one, or you are not sure whether a particular sub-clause is correct or not, etc. Your subconscious is not sure what to do, and so you are stopped dead. A related reason is indecisive thinking about your subject. You decide approximately what you want to say, and in making your outline it seems sufficient. But when you write, you realize suddenly that more thinking is required on a certain point; again, you are stopped.

You cannot discover these problems introspectively when they first occur, because your subconscious functions lightning fast, like a computer. It can grasp what you have not grasped consciously. That is, if you give your subconscious contradictory orders, it does not hold on to that contradiction; rather it instantly identifies the implication of contradictory orders—and shuts down.

Solving the squirms is perhaps the most painful part of writing. You must stop writing when they occur, but continue to work on the problem. To the best of my knowledge of psycho-epistemology, there is no other way out. The worst thing to do is to think that since it is a subconscious problem, you can take a rest, read a book, go to the movies—and let your subconscious resolve the problem. It will not. If you take a break of that kind, you prolong the agony. And the longer you postpone the problem, the less chance you have of solving it.

The problem *can* be solved, but it must be done consciously. You must sit at your desk and think about it, even when you feel you do not know what to think. For an exercise in free will and will power, this is the hardest thing you can demand of yourself, but it is the only solution.

As you consider the various aspects of the problem—what is the obstacle, what do you want to say, should you try another approach—you think of different ways of solving it, each one ending in a blind alley. But do not get discouraged; as you consider and discard various possibilities, you are actually untangling the knot in your subconscious.

If you have a tendency to feel unearned guilt, you will certainly feel it at the end of such a day. I never feel it, except in a state of squirms. But I know how to localize it. I know consciously that this is a technical, professional problem, and not a reflection on my self-esteem. Therefore, above all, do not take the squirms as an indication of your intelligence or writing talent or self-esteem.

While trying to solve the squirms, you feel as if you are accomplishing nothing. But in fact, while you struggle with the problem, you are eliminating confusions or contradictions in your mind. After three long days of work, for example, you may wake up the next day knowing you have to start the struggle again. You have no clue to the solution when you start on one more possibility, but *suddenly* you have the right idea. It is like a revelation from another dimension, though you know it is not. (This is one reason so many writers talk about inspiration from God or a spirit that moves the hand.)

You become eager to write and it goes beautifully. When your final attempt breaks through and clarifies everything, it is not an accident. It was made possible by those days of torture and false starts. That work was not wasted, even though at the time it felt as if it were.

You untangle the knot in your mind by eliminating wrong possibilities. Thus you have set your subconscious free to integrate, and the sudden "revelation" is the subconscious finally integrating the right elements. As Hutchinson points out in *How to Think Creatively*, it is like the accident of Newton's apple. He says that accidents happen to those who deserve them. He explains that if Newton had not worked on the law of gravitation, the apple falling on his head would have accomplished nothing. Newton had the knowledge, but was not yet able to integrate it. The apple falling on his head at the right time permitted the final integration of all that complex material. (I have heard that this apple story is not true. But true or not, it is the best illustration of the creative process; it applies equally to writing and every other creative activity.)

Solving the squirms requires integrating an enormous range of material, which may not happen immediately because of the number of wrong possibilities. Your mind can handle only so much at a time. At the right stage, however, one event can suddenly resolve the problem and reveal what kind of integration is necessary.

(Sometimes a writer has a personal problem unconnected to writing that he puts aside in order to write. He forces his mind away from the problem, yet it is more important to him than he realized. It occupies his subconscious, and therefore he has nothing to write with. If that happens to you, stop and solve the problem. As you gain experience, it will be easy to identify whether the problem is one of writing or a distraction from outside. The real squirms are those involving the writing itself.)

In *How to Think Creatively*, Hutchinson says he knows of no other solution to this problem than to keep trying and to remember that it is a necessary part of any creative process. He recommends that you maintain the conviction that you *can* solve the problem. I was startled when I read this, because I had reached the same conclusion through introspection. So far, there is no way known to avoid the squirms. But if you view them as a professional hazard and maintain your calm in the face of them, that is also the best way to foreshorten the torture. The reward, when it comes, is worth it.

If, however, you tell yourself you are no good, then you may not find a solution without the help of a psychologist. You are pouring oil on the fire. So do not doubt yourself.

"White Tennis Shoes"

A related problem is the pseudo-squirms or "white tennis shoes." Years ago I read an article in *The New Yorker* by a writer who described what she does in the morning before writing. What she describes is universal. When she sits down she knows she does not want to write. Here is what her subconscious does to "save" her from that difficulty. She thinks of everything she has to do. She needs to call a friend on business, and does so. She thinks of an aunt she has not called for months, and calls her. She thinks of what she has to order from the store, and places the order. She remembers she has not finished yesterday's paper, so she does. She continues in this way until she runs out of excuses and has to start writing. But suddenly she remembers that last summer (it is now winter) she never cleaned her white tennis shoes. So she cleans them. That is why I refer to this syndrome as the "white tennis shoes."

Getting into the writing state is difficult, and so you might procrastinate in this way. This is the pseudo-squirms: the normal reluctance to face an abnormal difficulty. This is not a moral, but a psycho-epistemological, issue. A mental switch is hard to make, yet it occurs every time you try to write, until you get used to writing and become severe with yourself. It is difficult to do because of the enormous concentration required. Every person has more than one value, and there are many legitimate things you could do which are easier than writing—maybe not cleaning tennis shoes, but going shopping or cleaning your apartment, for instance. Contrast these kinds of activity with a complete withdrawal from your total context and an intense concentration. The temptation to do something else is always there before you start writing.

In steelmaking, a blast furnace must be heated for weeks before it is hot enough to forge steel. A writer getting himself into the writing mood is like that furnace. Nobody likes to get into that state, though once you are in it you want no other, and would probably snap at anyone who interrupted you. Authentic squirms exist when there is a conflict: you cannot write, but neither can you take your mind off of writing. In such a state you could not think of tennis shoes. If the house were on fire you would not want to deal with it. But in the case of the "white tennis shoes," you must force yourself by sheer will power immediately to stop procrastinating and begin writing.

Let me mention another possible solution, which I learned from a good Hollywood writer. He told me that if he stops writing at the end of a sequence, it is difficult to pick up the continuity the next day. So when he reaches the end, he writes the beginning of the next sequence and then stops. I find this helpful sometimes, but it is not an absolute. If you come to the end of a sequence and know clearly where you want to go next, it is helpful to establish that beachhead for the next day's work. But if you have not thought out the next sequence (which is often the case), do not force yourself to go on.

Fatigue

A state between the squirms and the "white tennis shoes" is authentic fatigue. This occurs when you have been working for a long time, and so are too close to the subject and simply need a rest. The mind, like the body, needs rest. If you are struggling and your writing is stale and uninspired, take a break. Go to the movies, watch television, listen to music. Take your mind off the article, and come back to the subject with a fresh outlook.

Learn to distinguish your inner states. Decide whether you are feeling the squirms, or the "white tennis shoes" (where you simply have to exercise will power), or tiredness (when your mind is closed and will power will not do, since you would only be torturing an overloaded computer).

Circular Squirms

The difficulty in writing—both in planning an article and in executing it—is that it requires a strain in one's thinking, in the form of what might *appear* to be a contradiction.

Normally, as you acquire knowledge you automatize it. You do not hold all your knowledge in the same form in which you first learned it. Learning to speak is the best example; all other knowledge follows the same pattern. At first you learn words by conscious effort. You are in control of that knowledge when you no longer have to grope for words—when expressing yourself in words is so habitual that you cannot retrace the process by which you learned them. As an adult, you cannot grasp what happens in your mind when a thought is translated into words as you speak. But you can trace that process, as an adult, when you learn a foreign language. In groping for words in a foreign language, you can get an idea of what takes place in your mind when you first learn to speak. From that, you can see the real nature of automatization. First you learn something by focusing on it consciously. You have to grope for the knowledge and then use it consciously. With repetition and the growth of your knowledge, what you learn becomes automatized. It is not innate, though it feels that way. You have, quite properly, forgotten how you learned it, and all that remains is the result—the skill—which permits you to acquire further knowledge without having to stumble over words.

Knowledge is being automatized throughout your life (if you are not a case of arrested development). You are constantly increasing the complexity and scope of your knowledge. To the extent to which you are in command of that knowledge, you automatize it. For the purposes of further knowledge, you need not remember all the syllogisms you had to go through to be convinced of something. Your knowledge comes to feel like a self-evident primary, and you *use* it as if it were that; but if you are a good introspector, you know that it is not. This makes writing difficult. On the one hand, everything you know has become automatized. On the other hand, when you present your knowledge in writing, you must *break up* that automatization.

Often, you want to present a complex idea that is clear to you, and yet you cannot find the right words or do not know where to begin. A certain circularity seems to set in: you cannot present Point A without first explaining Point B, but Point B is not clear without Point A. This is natural. When you are in control of your subject, you hold it as an integrated, clear total. This is not subjective, but objective. But the *form* in which you hold it feels subjective, so when you try to explain it to somebody you do not know where to begin.

The remedy, in part, is to guard against the tendency to accept a conclusion while forgetting the road by which you reached it. If you know, for instance, that capitalism is the best system, you can surely remember that you did not always know it. There may even have been times when you were tempted toward other systems. The view that capitalism is best is a conviction acquired, at the earliest, on the semi-adult level, with full knowledge coming only later. But once you are fully convinced of it, you can operate with that knowledge automatically. If you read about a new law being proposed in Congress, you need not retrace all the reasons that once convinced you of the correctness of capitalism. Your mind automatically refers to your conclusion as a standard, and automatically evaluates some concrete law according to that standard.

But suppose that in the middle of such automatic functioning you suddenly questioned why you think capitalism is best. If such a doubt entered your mind seriously, you could not judge the concretes. The automatic circuits would be broken and you could not tell whether some law is good or bad. You would have to stop your machinery, in effect, and review the arguments that originally convinced you. If you met a liberal, you might find it difficult to show him that capitalism is best. It would be hard to organize your arguments, because you have forgotten the road you took intellectually to acquire this complex knowledge. You have retained, in conscious terms, only the conclusion—which is proper. But it is improper to let the underlying steps vanish from your mind entirely, because quite apart from writing articles or converting liberals, you may encounter new arguments or tricky political situations and find yourself helpless. As a general rule, try to remember at least the essentials of the process by which you arrived at a given conclusion, so that if you have to present that conclusion, you will have a standard for knowing what, in logic, is necessary to defend it.

What you must recall is the logical, not the biographical, process. You need not remember the actual thought process you yourself went through (though that sometimes helps). For an orderly epistemology, what matters is logic. For instance, if somebody told you that capitalism is the most productive system, that would not yet fully convince you. But if he pointed out that it is the only system that protects rights, or if he demonstrated that it is the only moral system, that argument will remain with you. This will enable you to know what is essential for a convincing article.

Remember the logical antecedents—the steps that convinced you of a conclusion, which you today regard as almost self-evident. Keeping track of these steps gives you a lead as to what to include in your article and how to delimit your outline. It will determine what is necessary to prove a certain point, and what are irrelevant details, elaborations, or side issues.

This difficulty particularly affects people who know their subject well. They know "too much," and thus the selection becomes difficult. When you have layer upon layer of complex integrations, and need to isolate a particular aspect within your specialty, organizing your article and delimiting your theme may be difficult. Whereas if, for instance, you write a spontaneous letter of indignation to your college newspaper—I never did in Soviet Russia, because we had no such newspaper, you can be sure—it may well be convincing. Though you know far less than you will later, within the confines of your knowledge you are making your point properly, since knowledge is contextual. But when you have "too much" knowledge, you can no longer do this so easily.

This does not mean that to write an article you must revise your entire method of thinking. I am merely giving you a lead to a possible cause of trouble. When you find yourself in the circular squirms—when you do not know where to begin because everything seems connected to everything else—take it as a sign of well-integrated, well-automatized knowledge, which may be causing problems because you did not retain the logical steps by which you arrived at it.

The solution is to break up the integration into its component parts, in logical order.

If you experience this trouble in the actual writing process, rather than in the outline, remind yourself that the circularity is only an illusion, and proceed. If you cannot decide whether Point A or Point B should be stated first, choose arbitrarily. If one is in fact better, you will discover that when you edit. But in your draft, do not hesitate over this kind of circularity for too long. If it stops you, make a quick decision and go on.

Editing Unwritten Sentences

An article, an outline, or a sentence does not exist until it is on paper. This is an absolute. It may seem obvious, but writers often ignore it and get into trouble. They act as if they can edit a sentence before it comes into existence.

Whenever your writing comes too slowly and you have to drag it out of yourself—sentence by sentence, or word by word—the error is that you believe a sentence exists in your mind or another dimension, and you can improve it before it exists in reality. But it does not exist. By existence, I mean objective reality, i.e., that which can be perceived by a human consciousness. That which exists in your own mind is only a state of consciousness. It is merely in the anteroom to existence for a creative work.

Do not judge your work, edit it, or discuss it until it exists on paper.

The same relationship exists between an embryo and an actual child. Catholics claim an embryo has the right to life, and that this supersedes the mother's life. This is a ridiculous misapplication of the concept of rights. Rights pertain to a baby which has come into existence, not to a mere potential. In the same way, the most beautiful future sentence, until it appears on paper, is only an embryo. (I have even heard people speak of a writer being "with novel." It is more than a metaphor.)

A work in progress does not yet exist. If it is a book, some chapters may exist, but the book itself does not. When you are writing an article, some paragraphs or sequences may exist, as you put them down on paper, but the article itself does not. The same principle applies to the building block of any writing: the sentence. A sentence does not exist until it is on paper. So let it be born before you decide that it is deformed or should be destroyed. Fortunately, one difference between writing and childbirth is that whereas you cannot destroy a child when it is born, a sentence (or entire draft) can be discarded if necessary.

The error of editing sentences before they exist occurs when, as you get a certain thought and begin putting it into words, you interrupt that crucial process and begin to edit. All beginners make that mistake, particularly conscientious ones. They think maybe they can make the sentence a little better.

There is a similar error people make. I know someone who went so far as to write down a sentence with great torture, and then consult a thesaurus, looking up every word to make sure there was not a better one. Then he would go on to the next sentence.

The mistake here is in thinking that a sentence can stand by itself, outside of any context. But remember that Objectivism, above any other philosophy, holds *context* as the crucial element in cognition and in all value judgments. Just as you cannot have concepts, definitions, or knowledge outside of a context, so you cannot judge a sentence out of context. All writing is contextual. The minimum standard, or unit of judgment, in regard to a sentence is its paragraph. But even that is not final because it depends on all the other paragraphs. Therefore, you cannot fully and finally judge the value of a sentence until you have finished the whole article (or, in a book, the whole chapter).

So do not edit sentences before they are on paper; and for the same reason, do not *immediately* start editing a sentence once it is on paper. Do not go to a dictionary, or wonder whether you should cut or add something, or whether it needs clarification. You cannot judge that until you see the total.

Over-staring

A corollary danger is too much rereading. In doing the draft, this occurs when you focus too much on a sentence, thereby losing your context and your direction. Then, to try to recover them, you constantly reread the preceding sentences. The result is that by the end of the first day of writing, you have memorized your paragraph. That is a problem all young writers suffer from.

The greatest danger in regard to control over your writing is to memorize your first draft. That sets it in your mind as the final expression of what you want to say. As a result, you lose the capacity to evaluate or edit it, which requires that you be able to take a fresh look at your material. That is why the earliest you should edit your work is the next morning; editing requires a switch to a conscious process, which is a different mental set.

If you *over-stare* at a passage (as I call it), you delay for an indeterminate period the time when you can properly edit it. You may struggle, by will power, to edit it, but you will be handicapped: you will hear only a memorized recital in your mind and will not be able to say whether it is good, effective, and eloquent. (The only time you should over-stare is when your article or book is in print. That kind of gloating is appropriate and enjoyable, and you can even learn from it.)

If you do over-stare, struggle by whatever means you can to forget your material. Go so far as to pretend that you have forgotten it and try for a fresh look. Sometimes you will have to put the article aside for a week or more. But you will actually gain time that way, because otherwise each time you try to edit, you will become blinder to it, and eventually lose interest.

Pet Sentences

Many writers save pet sentences from passages they have discarded, with the hope of putting them to use in another work. A writer, however, must make a conscious choice to write on a certain subject and theme, and then must program his subconscious for that job. If, on a given sequence, his mind is more concerned about using these brilliant pet sentences or aphorisms, it will not function properly, and he will torture himself. The reason is that he is interfering with his own subconscious and trying to write by a partially conscious process. It is tantamount to giving himself the following impossible order: "I want to present a new theory of economics, with which I must integrate ethics and epistemology—and I also have sentences A, B, and C that must be included." The subconscious is getting too many orders, and contradictory ones at that. It will simply stop functioning.

Keep in mind that no matter how good your pet sentences are, nothing is brilliant outside of a context. If the context and logical progression of your presentation permit one of those sentences, it will come to you automatically. Your subconscious will not forget it. If it does not come automatically, then it does not belong in the new structure; and you cannot rework a structure merely to feature a particular sentence. So let it go or put it down in a notebook. (It *is* pleasant to save good sentences even if you cannot use them. After *Atlas Shrugged*, I had a huge pile of discarded pages with sentences I liked. There were many good formulations, descriptions, and lines of dialogue that I wanted to save for future reference, though I found no use for them in the novel.)

Quotations

A related difficulty involves handling quotations. Writing an article that includes many quotations is a real strain, because it requires a constant switch between a conscious and subconscious progression of thought.

The best way to handle quotations is to decide, while working on your outline, where you will place them. Do not pile up a lot of quotations without a firm decision about where to use them. Otherwise you will constantly strain between writing and looking at those quotations, wondering whether you should use number one here or number three, etc. Even if you do decide in advance, when you come to a quotation you are interrupting yourself—since a switch to the conscious mind is required—and thus will experience a certain amount of strain. But the strain is minimal if the quotation comes when you are ready for it; all you have to do then is copy it and continue.

Incidentally, always copy the quote in your manuscript (unless it is too long) so that it becomes part of your writing. Your mind integrates the quotation, and this gives you a proper springboard from which to continue.

Some writers make the same mistake with quotations that others make with pet sentences. For example, Leonard Peikoff told me that when writing *The Ominous Parallels*,[2] he had a problem quoting Hegel. He had favorite quotations that did not quite fit a particular discussion, but they were so horrible philosophically—and thus so interesting—that he regarded them as gems, and was eager to put them in. The principle is the same as in the case of pet sentences: the requirements of your context come first. Do not sacrifice logical progression for some outside consideration, such as a favorite quote. If you can fit it in, fine—but do not force it.

I had a problem handling numerous quotations in my article "Requiem for Man,"[3] which deals with the papal encyclical *Populorum Progressio* (*On the Development of Peoples*). The subject of my article was the encyclical, and thus quotations played a central part. I had to select the quotations that conveyed the encyclical's point clearly and in essentials, while preserving the continuity of my own presentation. To object convincingly to the encyclical, I needed my own argument running through the quotations. In addition, I had to alternate between making an assertion about the Pope's view, supported by a quotation, and presenting a quotation, then arguing against it. It was a difficult job of organization, because I had to switch so often between writing and selecting quotes.

Here is how I did it. First I broke down the encyclical into its essential points; then with colored pencils I established a code matching each color with a particular subject. I marked each relevant

[2]*The Ominous Parallels: The End of Freedom in America* (New York: New American Library, 1982).
[3]*Capitalism: The Unknown Ideal.*

paragraph with the color pertaining to its subject. For example, red stood for economics, blue for politics, green for ethics, etc. Within each category, I selected only the most eloquent and essential quotations. I devised a system whereby each time I needed quotes on a given subject, I decided in advance which were best, and limited my choice to those. For instance, I started with the encyclical's view of capitalism. I had three or four marked in the appropriate color, looked up only those, made a quick decision, copied the quotation, and continued writing. I did the same for every other issue. That enabled me to integrate the reference material with the rest of my writing.

I prepared all this color coding before I made the final outline. I first made a tentative outline and organized the quotations, then I made a final outline in which I numbered the quotations, which were already categorized. As I proceeded to write, I could make quick selections according to those numbers. It was still difficult, but it was much easier than stopping each time and hunting through the encyclical for an appropriate quotation. So if you need to quote from research material, the principle is: select the best in advance, and confine your choice to those while writing.

You may find, when you reread your first draft, that you want to add or eliminate some quotation(s). This is relatively easy, and it is better to have to do this during editing than to give yourself too wide a choice, which leaves you open to too much hesitation during the writing process itself.

Mulling

The mulling-over period precedes all other stages of writing. It is a process of thinking in which you use your conscious mind to call forth certain ideas from your subconscious. It involves a tentative projection of a given subject and theme. How exactly the process will work depends on your mind, your interest in a given subject, and your familiarity with it. So there can be no rules about this process.

If you have notes, clippings, quotations, etc., that pertain to your theme, it is certainly helpful to look them over during this period, because that helps you integrate your material. But there can be no rules about how often or when precisely to do it. As a general practice, you will find that at a certain stage of this process you need to do some reading on your subject; that may stimulate your mind and help you to clarify your theme. But at another stage, it may be bad for you to read more, because that is when your subconscious needs to integrate the material already there. You have to acquire the right amount of knowledge, and then give your subconscious time to digest and integrate it. (Of course, if you still feel confused, you can always do further thinking and discover more material.)

In the mulling-over process, you—your conscious mind—are playing an instrument: your subconscious; and it is up to you to discover (by introspection) what your subconscious needs at which stage of writing. You must learn to trust the signals your subconscious gives you. If you order yourself to do more reading for a given article, but feel boredom and an enormous reluctance, it is likely that your subconscious already has what you need, and that further research is redundant or irrelevant. By contrast, say you project what you would like to convey in an article and even begin to make an outline, but you keep losing your train of thought, as if encountering patches of fog. Chances are you have not done enough thinking about, or research on, your subject. This is when you should look up more material or go over your notes again.

This is very general advice, because only you will be able to tell what is necessary in each case, which will vary from article to article.

Premature Discussion

As a rule, it is dangerous to discuss your future article with your spouse or friends before you finish your outline. Just as a sentence does not exist before it is on paper, neither does your article (not even as a potential) until you have clarified what you want to say. It does not become firm, even in your own mind, until you have an outline.

Before you make an outline, what exists in your mind is a creative nebula, not a solar system. It is a chaos of matter which *might* be organized into a solar system. In this, the mulling-over stage, you are vulnerable to any outside suggestions, precisely because you have not made up your mind fully. In order to write, you need more knowledge than you can include in any article, and while you are choosing what to include from that knowledge, you are vulnerable to outside influences.

There is no rule about how long the mulling-over process will last. It depends on your knowledge of the subject. Whether it is one day or several weeks, there is a period during which you are merely playing with the subject freely in your mind, and projecting in a flexible way what to include. This is how you condition your subconscious to that particular subject.

If you discuss your article while in this state, any suggestion seems to acquire a high level of objectivity, because it comes from outside. It is real—somebody has stated it—whereas your own view is still chaotic. The danger comes not from a bad suggestion, but from a *good* one. If the suggestion is bad, it might delude you temporarily, but eventually you will see through it. But suppose you are groping and somebody gives you a valuable suggestion which, however, comes from outside your own context. You may consciously grasp and agree with it, but you have not integrated it by yourself. Such a premature conclusion will act on your outline and future article in the same way a favorite quotation or sentence does. The outside suggestion becomes an absolute to which you must fit your article, and the result is a badly constructed piece. You will give birth to a crippled baby, with an extra leg or arm.

Let me tell you how I discovered this principle. I wrote a stage adaptation of *We the Living*, which was produced under the title *The Unconquered*. It was a flop. The idea of making *We the Living* into a play was not mine. A producer who had read the book approached me with the idea. He took an option on it, and I wrote the play. (In the end, he could not raise enough money to produce it, but about a year later, an actress became interested, approached me, and arranged for George Abbott to produce it.)

I had a terrible time writing the play, and I disliked every version

of it, from the original to the many rewrites. I became acutely aware
of the fact that my purpose in writing it did not originate with me.
In addition, my reason for writing it was to promote the book and
help publicize it. (The novel had been killed totally by the default
of the publisher; it went out of print after one edition of 3,000
copies.) So I had a legitimate motive—only it was not a literary
motive. My primary goal and interest were not in the play as such.

The play never was—and I came to realize, never could be—
good. It grew out of somebody else's suggestion plus my own irrelevant motive. So, no matter how conscientiously I tried, I could not
make it good. The final version was more or less competent, but no
better. This taught me never to write anything that was not my own
idea. Even if it is a good idea, if it does not come out of my own context, I will be unable to integrate it. It will not be first-handed.

Know when you are free to discuss a project. Before you start
preparing an article, it is all right to discuss the subject. An exchange of views may help you clarify your own ideas. Regard it as a
general discussion of ideas, not something you are engaging in with
an eye to your future article. But when you are preparing to work on
your outline and are still in the mulling-over stage, do not discuss
the subject or the article. Once you put your outline on paper and it
actually exists, then you can discuss it. You have formulated your
own integration and thus can judge whether or not you will be able
to use an outside suggestion. In short, learn to determine when discussion can be helpful, and when it can be confusing.

There are people who talk for years about the articles or books
they intend to write. Editors have a general impression, which is
true, that when a writer talks too much about a project, it will never
be written. Psycho-epistemologically, the reason is the same as in
discussing an outline too soon. If you discuss a project too much before it is clear in your mind, particularly a large project like a book,
you only confuse yourself.

In some cases the motives here are dishonest. I have in mind
those perennial novel-promisers who like playing the role of novel-
ist without bothering with the difficult job of writing. Psycho-
epistemologically, what helps the dishonesty along—or rather, what
penalizes it—is that the would-be writer's act dissipates his ability.

He confuses his subconscious by discussions with, and suggestions from, others, and he never gets to the actual writing. So even if he started with a semi-honest, vague intention to write that book, he can no longer do it.

Interruptions

If I get up in the morning and know, for example, that I have a four o'clock appointment, I cannot write that day. It is as if my mind closes down and will not work. If I do try to work, I dawdle, look at the clock, and get dressed for the appointment earlier than necessary, realizing that trying to write is useless. The psycho-epistemological reason is that in order to write, you must concentrate and keep your subconscious open, so that it will formulate the ideas you need. It is difficult to get into that state, and if you know that at a certain time—regardless of your progress—you will be interrupted, that knowledge will stop you completely. Implicitly, your subconscious says: "What's the use? All this effort for an hour or two. And *if* it goes well, that's when I have to cut it off." Therefore, I accept no daytime appointments unless it is absolutely unavoidable. (When I was writing *Atlas Shrugged*, I accepted neither day nor evening appointments, with rare exceptions, for roughly thirteen years.)

This, again, is like the blast furnace I mentioned, which must be heated for weeks before it is ready to forge steel. It is a disaster if the furnace goes out. A furnace not in use is still kept burning, because it is a long and expensive process to bring it back to the right temperature. This is a good metaphor for preparing the mind for writing, which takes such an enormous level of concentration that an interruption is like the furnace going cold. If you are interrupted, it takes much longer than the appointment to bring yourself back to work. Not only will you not work the same day, you will most likely lose the next day as well. This happens even to experienced writers who recognize their inner signs.

Do not attempt to write if you have urgent interruptions. If you can, set yourself certain days of the week during which you do nothing but write. Do all your other duties during the other part of the week. Subconsciously, what you need in order to write is that sense of an uninterrupted immediate future. It cannot extend forever, but you must know that at least for today—and preferably for the next few days—you will be free to devote yourself to writing alone.

Similarly, if you have a mixed profession (i.e., a job besides writing), it is better to divide your week into two parts than to attempt to do both jobs on the same day. Some people can manage it, but I have never been able to. When I worked at jobs other than writing, I could not write at night, but only on the weekends. Some people, however, are more elastic; a lot depends on your psycho-epistemology. But it is an absolute that you cannot work if you know that an interruption is imminent.

Deadlines

There is no general rule about deadlines. Whether they come from the outside or are self-imposed, they can be helpful or harmful. They are helpful if, for instance, you are writing a book, feel you will never finish, and have attended to none of the practical details— such as approaching a publisher. In such cases, the absence of a deadline can have a bad influence. You could spend the rest of your life adding chapter upon chapter. Writing is dependent on a complexity of psycho-epistemological issues, and the idea of an eternity before you is harmful. A *certain* pressure is necessary—the pressure of reality: if you are writing something, it is appropriate to finish it. So a deadline does serve a purpose.

However, if you *must* deliver a certain number of words on a given subject by a certain date, that too can be disastrous. You will either write carelessly, because you lack the time to think, or be completely paralyzed. The tendency is either to become a hack (writing only what comes to you easily) or not to write at all.

The important issue, however, is not outside deadlines, but self-imposed ones. The ideal condition for writing is to set aside time, work as you can, and not panic if a day passes without your producing something new. Nevertheless, you must set deadlines for yourself—not as absolutes, but to avoid concluding subconsciously that there is no time limit on the assignment. Making your project indefinite is demoralizing.

Do not make time a constant pressure. Do not judge your progress by each day; since the production of any written material is irregular, nobody but a hack can be sure how much he will produce in a given day. Otherwise, if you have a great, inspirational day and produce ten pages, you will tend to think: "At this rate, I will finish in a month." And if the next day is unproductive and you write a single dubious sentence, you might think: "At this rate, it will take me two years." Both are demoralizing illusions. If you have a bad day, it will add to your discouragement to project your own future at such a dismal pace. On the other hand, if you come to an unwarranted, overly optimistic conclusion, and feel you can write without difficulty forever, that is a temporary illusion. Your next bad day (often the following day, precisely because of this conclusion) you will be crushed, because you based your schedule on this fast, uninterrupted progression.

Do not make any time generalizations in that form. Writing is an unpredictable process; it does not proceed regularly at so many words per minute. You can judge your pace only in larger installments; your standard should be roughly the production of an average week. But there are always unpredictable factors. You may have personal problems, an illness, unavoidable interruptions—so do not set yourself such absolutes as: "I must finish in so many weeks or else I am no good." The absolute you *do* have to comply with is: "I will write during all the time that I can (or all the time that I set aside for writing) to the best of my ability." Only you will know when you did your best—even if you merely produced a paragraph—or when you dawdled all day. With experience, you acquire a special sense of this. Therefore, keep a general deadline in your mind, but without being too specific about the date. Do not put unnecessary pressure on yourself.

Duty

If you make something a duty, you will not be good at it. Creatively, acting on duty is a major barrier and destroyer.

If you write from a sense of duty—say, you do not want to write the article, but some publication needs it, or somebody wants you to do it, or you are doing it for "the cause"—then your motive is not the desire to say things about this subject, but some extraneous consideration. That is the duty premise, and it will cause you nothing but trouble. Usually, writing on a duty premise produces nothing but unnecessary squirms caused by a rebellious subconscious.

Apart from an outside duty, there is such a thing as *self-made* duty, which is, paradoxically, a passionate desire to write a given piece. It is so strong that you almost paralyze yourself. I experienced that while writing *The Fountainhead*, and I discovered the solution by accident.

Often, especially after I had gone through the squirms, I would get up in the morning and want desperately to write. But when I sat down, I felt blank. It was neither the squirms nor the "white tennis shoes." I could not think of anything but writing, and yet I could not write. In such cases, I played solitaire, simply to do something not very purposeful while my mind got used to the idea of writing.

One day, in this state, I picked up the cards. But I did not want to play, I wanted to write. I thought to myself: "Why don't you try it? This won't be writing yet, you will merely project what seems to be pressing on your mind." I left the cards on the table, and thought I would come back to them in a few minutes. I wrote for four hours, uninterrupted, and it was one of my best days of inspirational writing. That taught me something. By an overpassionate desire, I put myself in a state of self-made duty. It was not a duty to the cause, the book, the publisher, etc.; it was simply my own desire to write. But I made a duty out of it because I told myself that I *have* to write. Such intensity stopped me, and I realized that the cards, left there accidentally, helped me break the duty premise. They were a reminder that I could stop whenever I wanted—that I was writing only for myself. I grasped something very important, which is a solution to most writing problems (though it cannot solve deep squirms). It is what I call the pleasure principle.

When you feel overburdened by the problems I have discussed, one of the best solutions is to ask yourself what *you* want. You are not writing for the cause, for humanity, for posterity. You are writing because you *want* to write; and if you do not want to, you do not have to, neither today nor ever. Remind yourself that it is all for your own happiness, and if you truly dislike the activity, do not try it. Writing is too difficult to do with a half-intention.

Most people who try to write, however, really want to. Therefore, the best way out of technical difficulties—the best fuel psychologically—is to remind yourself, explicitly, that writing is for your own pleasure. Never mind your mistakes or who will say what about your work. Remind yourself what you sought in writing, and what great pleasure there is in having your say about life, reality, or whatever subject you choose.

In conclusion, I want to answer a question that may have occurred to you. If writing requires so many principles—so much philosophical knowledge—why are unphilosophical writers able to write (particularly in fiction)? For instance, Mickey Spillane has enormous imagination. His style is flawed, but he writes a novel in two weeks, inspirationally, and sends it to his publisher. He does not edit it, and he does not permit corrections.

Many people above him intellectually nevertheless have difficulties in writing. So how does he do it? The answer is: the same way a somnambulist is able to walk a tightrope, while you cannot. If, early on, you set your writing premises subconsciously and exempt the realm from any psychological or philosophical problems, you will be able to write. That is how writers even with inner conflicts can write, at times brilliantly. The danger, however, is that you are completely at the mercy of your subconscious, and cannot get out of the slightest psycho-epistemological difficulty. This is true of all inspirational writers. They cannot improve, and they soon write themselves out. If the material in their subconscious runs out, there is no way for them to replenish it, and thus they cannot develop. Such writers exempt the process of writing from conscious questions or premises. They rely entirely on the subconscious. The somnambulist on a tightrope moves with absolute certainty, focused only on his particular job. But if you awaken him, he will fall, because he cannot walk the rope consciously.

So if you have not learned how to write automatically, as Spillane does, and cannot put yourself in the state of a somnambulist's single-tracked assurance, your only alternative is to learn to write by a long, conscious process. After all, you *can* learn to walk a tightrope, though it must be done by conscious practice; and when you thus acquire the skill, it is *much* more reliable and pleasant than a somnambulist-like dependence on your subconscious. In the somnambulist's state, your writing and inspiration are not fully in your control.

Do not envy the "inspirational" writers. Learn the skill of writing consciously.

7

Editing

There are three major differences between writing and editing. First, in writing you rely on your subconscious with minimum interference from your conscious mind. In editing, you do the opposite: the dominant process involves your conscious mind.

Second, writing, unlike editing, must be highly personal. You go by your emotions, as if you were writing only for yourself. While writing, do not criticize or edit yourself. In editing, however, you must be as objective and impersonal as possible. Try to forget what you have written and read it as if it were by someone else. This is not difficult to do. Anyone who has acted or played charades knows that one can pretend to be another person. So imagine that you have forgotten how the article was written, including all of the emotions, hesitations, and choices involved.

Here is where memorizing your writing impedes you. If you have read your piece too often, you are helpless to edit it. When I wrote *We the Living*, it took me a week or longer before I could sufficiently forget a particular day's work and start editing it. I could not get a fresh look because I wrote too slowly and thus memorized everything. By the time I reached *Atlas Shrugged*, I could edit something the next day. That should be your goal.

You can make a few corrections the day you write, but I am speaking of editing as your main assignment. It is best to edit the next day. If you write steadily, you must reread what you have written in order to continue. And if you try to edit while you know every word, you might catch a few errors, but you will also memorize it more firmly; by the time you finish the sequence or the article, you will not be able to judge anything. If you cannot tell what is good or bad about an article, you have over-stared. So if you cannot be objective the next day, do not start editing. Edit only when you know you are ready.

Third, while writing, you must not question anything or doubt yourself. While editing, however, you are free to question *everything*, including whether to reconstruct the article totally or even whether to continue with it at all.

Do *not*, however, start doubting for doubting's sake. This is a common error; it is part of the mistake of thinking you must write the "perfect" article. If, as you edit your article, it seems good, but you think: "I don't see any error, but what if I could do better?"— that can paralyze your judgment. The epistemological principle is that *the zero does not exist*. Just as in science you need some evidence to warrant a hypothesis, so in judging what you have written you should not ask: "I do not know how it could be improved, but what if it could be?" Question everything, but do not raise unwarranted doubts.

In editing, there are two principles you must remember: (1) no judgment can be made out of context; and (2) you cannot do everything at once. Therefore, the subconscious also plays a part in editing, though you have to know how to use it. I recommend *editing in layers*, i.e., in several stages, by going over your first draft many times, from different aspects.

Let me explain the overall process of editing (i.e., the procedure for a completed article) and then how to apply it to the kind of editing you may want to do on a given part of an article.

First, reading your article, focus mainly on structure. Ask yourself: Is the logical progression good or confused? Are there repetitions? Is there imbalance, i.e., are some aspects too detailed and others too brief or condensed? (Not all aspects need to be equally detailed; you determine this by your theme and purpose.)

These are the types of questions you should ask during your first layer of editing. The answers will determine whether you should rearrange the article's structure or let it stand. No matter how carefully you prepare your outline, the actual execution may show that you did not select the best logical order and that some passages should be transposed; for example, certain points may be clearer or more dramatic if they come earlier. So in editing, focus on structure first. There is no use bothering about style or polish if you are going to have to reconstruct the article.

If, while you focus on structure, stylistic or grammatical corrections happen to occur to you spontaneously, then make them. For example, if in some passage you see immediately that there are too many adjectives, or a better adjective occurs to you, make the change. But if you notice that something is wrong stylistically, and the correction does not occur to you immediately, do not work on it during the first reading. Make a mark in the margin and continue focusing on structure.

Incidentally, do not let your outline show in your article. Do not let the reader in on the mechanics of what you are doing. Always let him in on the content, of course, but not on the scaffolding. The mistake here takes the following form. As you finish a sequence, you write, for instance, "So much for aspect A, now we will discuss aspect B." That is the scaffolding, and you should remove it. These are directions written for yourself; they are what you put in an outline. Your outline indicates that you must cover Point 1, then Point 2, etc., but in the actual writing, if the structure of your article is logical, you need not announce that you have finished Point 1.

Once you are satisfied with the structure, read the article again. In the second reading you should focus on clarity of thought and content. That is, on the first reading, you assume the content is clear. As long as you know what you are writing about, you can judge the structure. But on the second reading, you examine the verbal part of your writing—sentence structure and content—very carefully. Watch for the clarity with which you express your thoughts and whether the words you use objectively reflect what you want to say. Ask yourself explicitly: "Do I really know what I want to say, and have I said it?" Frequently you will answer in the negative. Later I will discuss the errors possible in this category.

Only on the third reading should you focus on style. Again, I will discuss the details later. Here I simply want to point out that you should not worry about saying something in a more interesting way earlier than the third reading. As you acquire experience, ideas for presenting things more colorfully will occur to you all the time—in your original draft and in the first two editings—because your subconscious will have the necessary standing order. But do not force this. Do not consciously focus on style until the final editing.

Do not take "three readings" too literally. There is no rule about how often you need to read your article. You may be able to combine some of the functions of the three readings into two. More likely, you will need many more than three. Do not take the number of readings you need as a reflection on your abilities. If you know a great deal, you might need ten readings fully to accomplish everything. There is only one general principle, which each of you must apply individually: you cannot do everything at once, because too much is involved. You must edit in *layers*, according to how much your mind can handle at one time. This in turn depends on your experience, and on your knowledge of and interest in the subject.

Here is how I myself discovered the process of editing in layers. I had always edited in that way, but I never understood the principle involved until I wrote for the *Los Angeles Times*. I had to write a weekly column[1] of no more than a thousand words, though I was told a length of 700 to 800 words was preferable. Of course, I first made an outline, then wrote the draft, and then edited it. As I went over it once, I discovered that cuts were always possible; but then I would come to the point where I felt nothing more could be cut. This seemed fine, because I was a bit under a thousand words. But to my amazement, the next time I read the piece I could cut some more, and the next time still more, until I got the word count down to around 750. I did this without straining after anything new, and

---

[1] See *The Ayn Rand Column*, edited by Peter Schwartz (Gaylordsville, CT: Second Renaissance Books, 1991; expanded ed., 1998).

without cutting content. What impressed me most was that I could not have made all these cuts in the first editing. That made me grasp the extent to which a mind cannot do everything at once.

When you first read your article, you see only the obvious cuts. But after you eliminate them and read it again, in that new context you can see that other changes are necessary. For example, some sentences are too long, or there are two adjectives where only one is needed, or there is an unnecessary subordinate clause that was needed in the first version, but not in the edited one.

Incidentally, because the *Los Angeles Times* left it up to me, I took pleasure in being as economical as possible without spoiling the content. It became a challenge and a good exercise.

I grasped the principle—that you cannot do everything at once—on merely one aspect of writing: brevity. When you consider all the elements of writing—from your subject and theme, to eloquence of expression—you see that you cannot possibly hope to do everything the first time you edit. If you try, you are asking the impossible of your mind.

Learn the rate of work—the tempo—appropriate to you, and then adjust it according to each job; the principle is that you must concentrate purposefully, since you cannot do something in part focus, but you must not strain. What stops you is demanding the unnatural of your mind. When you feel an inner tension, that may be a sign that you are trying to do too much and need to put the work aside for a while. Later, go back to it with a fresh mind. A mind can do only so much at any one time; be careful not to overwork it.

How do you know when something in your writing is wrong? In my article "Art and Sense of Life,"[2] I point out that your subconscious integrates data much faster than you can do so by a conscious process. It integrates all the elements of your article as you read it. Therefore, as you edit, if you leave your subconscious free, you will feel uneasy over an error before you consciously discover the error. You feel something is wrong, but cannot immediately say what it is. Part of the experience you need in editing is to discover the form in which your subconscious tells you that something is wrong. Discover

[2] *The Romantic Manifesto.*

those inner signs, which you alone can recognize. Sometimes merely identifying that there is something wrong enables you to discover the exact nature of the problem. At other times, the discovery can take a long time. It depends on the complexity of the error.

Refusing to engage in doubt for doubting's sake will help you preserve your natural, subconscious integrations. Self-doubt stifles the authentic subconscious warning that something is wrong. Since you cannot always discover what is wrong immediately, if you introduce too many doubts—e.g., the fear that there is some error because "it's poor little me who's writing, and I don't know how"—you will *constantly* feel that something is wrong and will not be able to judge your article properly.

If you approach editing objectively, you have nothing to fear. If there are mistakes in your piece, you or your editor will find them. If you are stuck on a problem and have exhausted your ability to solve it, an objective check is always possible. An editor, or even an intelligent friend, can tell you what is wrong, because he comes to the problem with a fresh mind.

Sometimes when you work too long on a passage, you become unsure about it, so you edit and change it. Then two days later, you restore the original version. I call this over-improving, and it usually occurs because you did not rest enough to be objective about your article. This is a normal part of editing, so do not worry about it.

There are two kinds of changes that are always appropriate to make right away. First, if anything comes to your mind spontaneously—e.g., a better word or a better sentence structure—make the correction, no matter what layer of editing you are doing. Second, make any correction which can be done relatively briefly. For example, on a complex paragraph, you may spend about half an hour. You may think over what is unclear, or try different ways of saying something. This is no longer spontaneous; it requires purposeful thinking. But if you spend two hours on one paragraph, you are on the wrong track. Here, time is proof of something. If you find that you need to think over every adjective or to reformulate a sentence in ten different ways, and the more you try the more confused you become, then put the work aside until you can trust your subconscious to correct the problem.

During this type of self-torture, it may appear that you are being extremely conscientious, because you keep trying, no matter how painful it is. But it is actually self-indulgence. You are being stubborn and acting, in effect, as if there were a battle between you and a sentence.

It occurs when you attempt to solve a problem out of context. You are stumped by a particular sentence—but maybe your subconscious is telling you that the whole paragraph is unnecessary. Or your mind simply wants to go on and not bother with this at present. In such cases, do not keep struggling with the sentence word by word, because it will delay you in two ways: first, you will not solve the problem, and second, you will exhaust your mind. You will become tired not only of the sentence, but of the whole article; and consequently you may find yourself unable to work on it productively. You will have exhausted your creative potential, and so will need time to rebuild your enthusiasm. Therefore, in this position, stop, trust your subconscious, and take a wider look at your article.

By taking a wider look I mean: leave the problem passage alone and begin another layer of editing. Read the article from another aspect, and by the time you come to the problem passage again, something might occur to you. If it does not, go on, edit everything else, and leave that passage to the end. If, however, you refuse to leave that passage until you have fully figured out how to redo it, you will legitimately begin to hate writing, because such a process is torture. The problem, however, is neither in the content of your writing nor in your talent, but in your use of the wrong method. Do not attempt anything by forcing your mind. Learn what *it* requires. Consciously observe what your mind needs in order to work hard, purposefully, and with great concentration—but without strain.

Do not edit word by word. Moreover, do not use a thesaurus. That is sometimes handy at the very end, for a final polish, but not until then. Use the best of what your subconscious can do in the easiest and most purposeful way possible.

My method—edit first for structure, then for clarity of thought and content, then for stylistic trimming—is only a general subdivision. Find whichever method is best for you. Although you must edit for structure first and style last, you may subdivide editing in many different ways, and require more than one reading for each subdivision.

The general process of editing can be applied to a book or article as a whole, as well as to their parts. For instance, in *Atlas Shrugged* I went over each sequence of a chapter by this three-step method, then the whole chapter, then each of the three major parts of the book, and finally, the whole book. If you do not strain while editing, your subconscious keeps the full context—what you have written and where you are going—constantly present in your mind, thereby enabling you to find many things to smooth out, clarify, or eliminate. Because I was not straining, it was an easy process, and progressively I had less and less to change. But the method I used was always the same, no matter what unit of writing I was editing.

No one can write an article in a day. So as you begin work each day, you should reread the work of the day before. Of course, the desire to edit will be irresistible, and this is appropriate; you want to bring order to your previous day's work before you proceed. But here I strongly recommend that you focus only on structure and clarity (plus whatever occurs to you spontaneously). Check your previous day's work *only* to see that its logical progression is appropriate and that your sentences and paragraphs are clear. If you do more than that, you open yourself up to a further handicap. You bring your previous day's work to a high polish, you are pleased with it, you feel inspired at seeing how beautiful your work can be—but now you have to start on your raw material of the second day. Instead of being inspired, you feel discouraged.

I went through this process and know it is unavoidable. It is like going from a beautifully polished, civilized city back into the jungle—back to the first draft. But you do not want to go back, and you get angry at yourself. Your subconscious feels: "Well, if I wrote that beautifully, why can't I do it the first time?" (If you experience that emotion, you are forgetting that it took you at least two days—the first draft and one morning of editing—to arrive at that smoothness; you cannot write that way the first time.) So do not over-polish the preceding day's work. Do full polishing only after finishing a sequence. If you could leave your whole article in an unfinished stage before starting to polish, then editing would be easier. But I do not recommend this, because the desire to polish each sequence right after it is written is unavoidable.

Now let's consider some other possible mistakes. There are two errors you need to watch out for, especially during the second layer of editing. The first is the failure to say what you thought you said; the second is ungrammatical writing.

The first is a complex issue, because it involves much more than writing, namely, objectivity. If you are at all subjective in your approach to life—in dealing with people or in expressing yourself—it will show up in your writing to an even greater extent. If you do not know what is required to make your ideas objectively clear, you will certainly have this problem when you write.

I cannot cure you of subjectivity. I can only indicate what it consists of and point out a few principles you can use in judging your work. Most important, try to read your article as if it were written by someone else. To the extent to which you have not formed objective premises about communication, you will find this difficult. Still, you must try your best.

The source of this problem is your need to know much more than the material you use in your article. When you confront that vast amount of information in your subconscious, the danger is that you will think you have made a certain point when you have merely approximated it; the rest of what you need to say is still in your mind. The penalty for subjectivism is the inability to distinguish between what is on paper and what is only in your mind.

As an editor of others, I often come to a sentence or paragraph and fail to understand it, because it can be read in different ways. When I ask the author what he means, he usually gives a brief and clear explanation—except that no part of that explanation is on paper. When I ask why he did not write precisely what he said, the answer is usually that he thought he had. When I point out that he has not, he sees that I am right, though he was incapable of discovering it himself. I cannot cure an error of this kind here. But to identify it is helpful, because you must explicitly ask yourself if what you have said is only an approximation; a lot depends on this.

Proceed as if you are writing a legal contract and as if every word will be held against you. When you write a contract, you must be careful about every adjective and comma. If something is unclear, disaster can follow. You should not even sign contracts for magazine subscriptions without reading the fine print. You must understand to what you are committing yourself. The same principle applies, in a different form, to writing. Look at the job of editing as if it were a review of a contract with reality. You must know that you have said exactly what you mean—no more and no less—and that it cannot be misunderstood.

Never sacrifice clarity. This is why the color of expression and the clarity of thought should be two separate jobs. If you are unsure of the clarity of some thought, never try to hide it by means of a jazzy twist or beautiful metaphor. It will not save your reader from confusion.

By the way, do not confuse clarity and precision. To be precise means to be clear in detail; it involves more than clarity. You can express a thought clearly, but it may not be fully precise. For example, if you say, "Man is good," that is clear—only one would not know exactly what you mean, because it is too broad an abstraction. If you then specify and say, "I regard man as good when he is rational," you have made it much more precise. It is an issue of the degree of abstraction.

Clarity applies to any level—to the broadest statement or to the minutest details. Whatever you say, it has to be clear. But precision is the issue that you have to consider when you are dealing with some abstraction and you have to decide whether, in your context, it requires more details (something closer to the concrete). Here again the subject and theme determine the level of abstraction. By the context of your writing, you have to decide when a statement, which may be clear, is nevertheless too broad (and will therefore be read as a floating abstraction).

There is, however, also a problem of over-precision. You may include a lot of unnecessary details, and thus dilute your clarity. This will cause the reader to lose the overall integration or the overall abstraction. Therefore, the issue you have to watch constantly—and have to automatize in your mind—is: when can you make an abstract statement and when do you need more details? Avoid both the error of floating abstractions, where the tie to concrete reality is lost, and the error of concrete-boundedness, where the abstraction is lost.

Here are two reasons why you might be unable to judge the clarity of your writing.

One is the attempt to overcondense. For example, you try to make two or three different points at once by means of imprecise generality. This is not the same as stating a wide abstraction, which subsumes many concretes, but still says *one* thing (which is what abstractions are for). The mistake I have in mind is taking two or more different points, or distinct aspects of a given point, and forcing them into one sentence. The result is the kind of sentence that drives an editor crazy. It seems to mean something important, but no matter how often he reads it he cannot tell exactly what it means. He has only an approximate sense of the author's intention. When he asks the author, he finds, say, that there are three distinct thoughts that should have been expressed in three separate sentences. But if you go step by step as your particular thought requires, not only will you be clearer, you might discover that you do not need all of the points that you tried to squeeze into that one sentence.

Another example of the attempt to overcondense is what I call the Germanic method of writing—making one enormous sentence out of what should be three or four.

A second reason you might be unable to judge clarity involves what I have said about automatization. If a thought is thoroughly automatized in your mind, and you do not know how to explain it or how to break it up, you might put it down only approximately. You believe it is objectively there on paper when it is not.

My advice in both of these cases is to proceed more slowly. When you feel you are squeezing a great deal into a short sentence, take that as a sure sign that you need to do the opposite. Write more slowly, perhaps even in more detail than you need. You can always cut later. But first get it fully and clearly on paper.

The second error I said you need to watch for when you edit concerns grammar. The relationship between objectivity and grammar is really a subdivision of the point about judging what one has written.

I regret that one has to discuss this with educated adults, but most

Americans do not know English grammar. It is all the more ridiculous coming from someone like me with a Russian accent. I do not mind the other errors in writing so much, but this one is the hardest for me to encounter, to work with, and to correct, because it represents a cultural phenomenon, and you are not responsible for it—the educational system is.

Americans are trained (through the look-say approach to reading and all allied, Dewey-based ideas of education) to be emotional approximators. The nonobjective, ungrammatical way in which people express themselves today is truly frightening. What has been systematically undercut is their capacity for objective communication. Americans tend to express themselves guided by feelings, not by thoughts. According to modern theory, there are no such things as thoughts; and even if there were, they could not guide us.

I am not a grammarian by profession. I do not know the grammatical rules of English by name, only by practice. But whenever I struggle with a sentence and finally get it straight, I bless whoever invented these rules and I know there is a reason behind them. If they were irrational, they would not survive. Sometimes grammarians do attempt irrational, arbitrary rules; but people do not abide by rules that complicate communication rather than clarify it.

One of the most important applications of the Objectivist attitude toward reason is grammar. The ability to think precisely, and thus to write precisely, cannot be achieved without observing grammatical rules.

Grammar has the same purpose as concepts. The rules of grammar are rules for using concepts precisely. Since sentences consist of concepts, the whole secret of grammar is clarity and the avoidance of equivocation. The grammar of all language tells us how to organize our concepts so as to make them communicate a specific, unequivocal meaning. If you compare the number of concepts we have with the vastly greater number of phenomena we deal with and have to describe by means of those concepts, you will grasp the importance of grammatical sentence structure.

If it were not for grammar, we could have words but could not speak sentences. We could merely say, for example, "Me Tarzan, you Jane." That is the nature of primitive languages. Civilized languages, by contrast, have a grammar precisely because we deal with more than first-level, perceptually based concepts. If you have to deal with the abstract—with abstraction from abstractions[3]—you must know in what order and by what rules to organize them in order to communicate a specific thought.

We were all bored by grammar in school. Memorizing rules is very dull. But by the time you reach college, you should realize how important those rules are. Therefore, if you know why we should fight for reason, and for the right view of concepts, then let us—on the same grounds—have a crusade for grammar.

Make it a rule to know sentence structure—to know which form communicates a thought and which is open to ten different readings—and you will understand the importance of grammar, not only for writing, but for cognition in general. You have to *think* grammatically. Do not accept ideas half in words and half with the feeling: "I kinda know what it means." Formulate what you think, and why, in specific words, even when you are alone. This is why it is advisable, if the thought is too abstract, to make notes. When you make notes, you are obliged to put the thought into an objective form—not for your reader, but for yourself. Always reduce your convictions to a verbal formulation of your own. That is the first step toward grammatical clarity in your thinking, and toward making grammar and precision a habit.

The difficulty here is that most of you today are so used to a subjective shorthand that you lose the distinction between your own inner context and an objective statement. It is permissible to use a mental shorthand in thinking, if it is clear to you. But a stenographer would be of no value if she could not transcribe her shorthand into a document in English. Similarly, when it comes time to write, you must translate your shorthand into objective language.

If you have forgotten your grade school lessons, get a good primer on grammar—preferably an old one—and revive your knowledge.[4]

---

[3]See chapter 3 ("Abstraction from Abstractions") of *Introduction to Objectivist Epistemology*.

[4]In her course, Ayn Rand does not recommend any specific primers on grammar. She does, however, recommend a more advanced work, H. W. Fowler's *A Dictionary of Modern English Usage* (Oxford: Clarendon Press, 1926; not to be confused with the third edition of Fowler, currently in print, which is quite different).

You will be surprised how much more important it appears to you now than it did when you were a child. The reason is that today, in reading those dry rules, you know why they were formed and why they are rational.

As to what your attitude toward writing should *not* be, the best image is "Ike the Genius" in *The Fountainhead*—the modern playwright who says he is a creative genius, not a typist.[5] Too many people today think: "I'm a creative genius, I'm above grammar." But nobody who thinks or writes can be above grammar. It is like saying, "I'm a creative genius, I'm above concepts"—which is the attitude of modern artists. If you are "above" grammar, you are "above" concepts; and if you are "above" concepts, you are "above" thought. The fact is that then you are not above, but far below, thought. Therefore, make a religion of grammar.

Apart from a review of grammar by means of a good primer, I would suggest the following. When a sentence of yours seems dubious, ask yourself some simple questions, such as: What is the subject and what is the predicate? Do the kind of grammatical analysis you did in school. You will be surprised at what you discover. For example, you may find that you switched grammatical subjects in midsentence. Also ask yourself whether your sentence has more than one meaning. Here you need the full context of your work, which is why I recommend you do this during the second stage of editing. Try to keep in mind the full implications of any generalized statement you make as you read it. Be sure not to state in the form of a general principle something you mean much more narrowly—an error that many beginners make, particularly when they deal with complex subjects.

Here are some examples of the two errors I have discussed, the failure to say what you think you said and ungrammatical writing.

The first two examples come from articles I edited for *The Objectivist*. One contributor wrote that "the government-sponsored critics want the public to accept modern art, not to understand it, because

---

[5] In *The Fountainhead*, the drama critic Jules Fougler says, "Your typing is atrocious, Ike," to which Ike replies: "Hell, I'm not a stenographer, I'm a creative artist" (p. 469).

it cannot be understood in rational terms." But this implies that one *can* understand modern art *irrationally*. This is an example of an unintended implication. Another contributor wrote: "Vast sums were spent, motivated by the desire for prestige." This is what a rushed job can do. Although the author's intention is clear, the sentence reads as if sums of money were motivated by the desire for prestige. "Sums" is the subject, but sums cannot be motivated.

Another, more philosophical type of error is one I caught in the first editing of my article "What is Romanticism?"[6] I originally wrote that the modern literati's resentment toward plot was "too violent for a mere issue of literary canons. . . . This type of reaction pertains to *metaphysical* issues, i.e., to issues that threaten the foundations of a person's entire view of life." The problem is that I am talking about today's literati. But if I left the line this way, I would be making a general statement that was wider than I could possibly intend— namely, that if someone ever feels that the foundations of his metaphysics are threatened, he will necessarily feel a virulent resentment. So what I did was add, in parentheses, "if that view is irrational," which was all I meant, and all that was necessary.

As another example, consider the error I committed in the original version of *Night of January 16th*.[7] I wanted to make a certain line extra strong, so I had Nancy Lee Faulkner leap up and yell, "It's a fictitious lie!" Many people read this, but nobody noticed the error until we were in rehearsal in a Hollywood production, and a friend of one of the actors pointed it out to me. I was shocked and grateful— the latter because I never made that mistake again. Originally, I made the mistake because I wanted to indicate that it was a very big lie—but what is a *non*-fictitious lie? So know what you have actually said, and discover whether it is what you meant to say.

Along the same lines, watch your punctuation. I am afraid that every writer is somewhat at fault here (except for Leonard Peikoff, who is more severe than I am). If you feel you are above grammar, then you will certainly feel you are above punctuation. But punctu-

---

[6]*The Romantic Manifesto.*

[7]The definitive edition of this play (first performed in 1934) is *Night of January 16th* (New York: New American Library, 1985).

ation is extremely important. Although there is a great deal of latitude in English, it is a language in which punctuation is particularly crucial. Incidentally, the other two languages I know—Russian and French—are not quite so prone to equivocation or double meaning. English is very condensed and exact (which is why I love it), but these very qualities make possible sentences that can be read in two different ways, according to whether you insert or omit a comma.

There are certain rules of punctuation that are optional, but the overall rule is to aim at clarity. Do not leave punctuation up to the editor or copyreader. Make a point of focusing on it and being firm on where you want a certain mark. For the purpose of clarity, it is advisable to know the purpose of your punctuation—to know what you want to separate from what.

Here is a ridiculous example of bad punctuation, which I came across years ago in *The New Yorker*, when that magazine collected (in the "Beautiful Clause Department") quotations from actual letters, articles, and books. This one illustrates the importance of the comma. The sentence, without commas, reads: "Many is the time I've driven down this lane with my beloved wife who has since gone to heaven in a buggy." Now you know what the author meant, but commas would have saved him: "Many is the time I've driven down this lane with my beloved wife, who has since gone to heaven, in a buggy." (Obviously, it is simpler to say "I have driven down this lane many times in a buggy with my beloved wife, who has since gone to heaven." But assuming the author wanted it his way, only commas could make the thought intelligible.)

I once heard of a politician who committed political suicide when he put up the following campaign billboard: "My opponent has had eight years at the public trough. Now give me a chance." What he meant was "give me a chance to clean it out" or "give me a chance in office." When such an error is committed in politics, the intent is usually obvious. The very ludicrousness of the statement saves it from confusion. But when it happens in a philosophical passage, it may not be so obvious. The same kind of double meaning, which is not immediately apparent, can be disastrous in articles that communicate ideas. So watch your grammar and your punctuation.

If you want to express your ideas, particularly ideas based on

Objectivism, learn clarity—and that means concepts, grammar, punctuation. I would rather have a simple, primer clarity than the best metaphors in the world. Make clarity a fetish, an absolute, a dogma, a god.

If you do that, everything else will be child's play.

8

Style

Style is a distinctive, characteristic mode of execution. This definition applies to nonfiction writing as well as to all other creative activities, and it encompasses everything pertaining strictly to the form in which ideas are presented.

Style cannot be done to order. This is an absolute. If, when beginning a sentence, you ask whether it is colorful, you will not finish it. Or you will produce one artificial sentence after two hours of work. Style is the result of subconscious integration. You can know in principle how to bring about stylistic trimmings, but you cannot make them to order. Style, therefore, should not be pursued consciously; so many elements are involved that no mind could attend to and integrate all of them. It must be left to your subconscious.

Style in this respect is somewhat similar to emotions. You cannot order yourself to feel (or not feel) an emotion. You cannot control your emotions directly. You can, however, control them indirectly by identifying their root. Emotions are not primaries; they have subconscious intellectual causes. The same is true of style, which comes from a value-integration and must occur spontaneously.

But your subconscious must be free enough to generate style. When writing, if you try to attend simultaneously to your outline, to the content of what you are saying, *and* to saying it elegantly, your subconscious will be unable to handle it all at once. When what you want to say is clear, however, then spontaneously you will find a way of saying it with a twist. So do not force yourself.

Colorful writing is important. It makes your thought clearer and more dramatic, and therefore has both an intellectual *and* emotional appeal to the reader. But there is nothing worse than forced colorful writing, e.g., stretched metaphors that do not quite fit the content. The result of forced color is that the reader will mistrust your content, even if you are otherwise logical and honest. Every reader can sense this. He may not be able to tell you why, but he will know something is phony.

The reason why a mannered, artificial style leads to phoniness is implicit in the definition of style. Style is a distinctive, characteristic mode of execution. Characteristic of whom? Obviously, of the writer, or else it is not an individual style. And distinct from what? Obviously, from that of others. But you cannot, by conscious calculation, write in an individual way that is different from that of everybody else.

A fact has been observed in literary circles which nobody can explain (but then these people explain so little): namely, that occasionally a writer appears who has no training, yet writes brilliantly. In the twenties there was a truck driver, with a commensurate type of education, who wrote quite well. I was not fond of what he wrote, but he was successful. What was good about his writing was that it was completely natural. He wrote the way thoughts came to him. That created an inner conviction in his manner of writing. It sounded authentic and original, because he obviously knew no literary rules. He often departed from convention, but these departures made sense.

On the other hand, a great many failed would-be writers are college-educated (and usually come from English departments). The reason they fail is obvious. Those who went to school in the past few decades were intimidated and stymied. They were given either too many wrong rules, or no rules at all—only mystical implications, such as "either you have it or you don't." They spent their time analyzing metaphors and senseless nonessentials. Instead of being helpful, these schools paralyze or discourage their students. But a truck driver may be free, if he has independently accepted certain premises, to express himself authentically and colorfully in his own way. This is one way in which education, particularly in the arts, can destroy rather than help potential talent.

You cannot develop a style consciously. But you *can* give your subconscious the standing order that you like stylistic color and want it to occur when possible. Be conscious of that desire, because you will not develop your own style if you never think about the subject. Whenever you read someone else's work, if you see something you like, identify it consciously. Say, "This is an interesting way of saying something; I like this." Then forget it. Do not memorize it, and certainly do not stock your subconscious with future, unintended acts of plagiarism. You would simply be stealing someone else's concretes. But each time you identify such a concrete, it is a renewed order to your subconscious that you like colorful writing. If possible, identify also the principle the writer used—and then forget it. Similarly, when you read a passage you regard as bad, identify that, and why you regard it as bad. By making such literary value judgments, you develop the subconscious premises from which your own style will come.

You will find that, unexpectedly, your mind will, for example, throw you the right metaphor. This is why many writers think style is an inspiration, when actually your subconscious is merely delivering after you have given it sufficient material and the permission to do so. Style comes from lightning-like integrations which your subconscious can make when it is free to do so. That is why you must write your first draft as spontaneously as possible, neither aiming at jazzy touches nor censuring yourself for their absence. When you forget about stylistic touches, they will come—sometimes in the first draft, and especially in editing. Instead of saying, "The cat is on the mat" (which is ideal for what it says), you might write, "A ray of moonlight fell from the silver fur of a cat, who sat on . . ." etc.—and you can do much better.

If you practice this kind of premise-setting, you will be surprised how observations that you forgot come out automatically. This is how you train your subconscious to throw you the right words in the right combinations when you need them, i.e., to suggest a form of expression which corresponds to your values.

As encouragement, let me tell you about my first published work, a pamphlet about the movie actress Pola Negri.[1] I was twenty and living in Soviet Russia.

At that time (in the twenties) American movies were beginning to appear in Russia, and they were very popular. Although there were no Russian fan magazines, some people could get American ones from friends and relatives abroad, and they were a treasure to us. A state publishing house for the cinema was publishing a series of monographs on foreign movie stars, and I asked if the house wanted to publish one on Pola Negri. She was a big star, and popular in Russia. I chose her because she was my favorite. They were delighted and commissioned me immediately.

After I submitted my first version of the pamphlet, the editor said I had good material, but that I wrote in a flat, dry manner that read like a synopsis. He asked if I could make it more colorful, but I did not fully understand what he meant. So he gave me a copy of the Max Linder pamphlet in the series—Max Linder was one of the first comedians on the screen, and was famous in Europe—and told me to observe how the author handled the material.

I read the pamphlet and was impressed. The author had done a beautiful job, precisely from the aspect of color. He never said anything in a dry, synopsis style, but neither was every sentence fancy. What he did was dramatize everything. Rather than write, "Max Linder was born in such and such year in Paris," he would say, "On such and such a spring day, a child was born to Mr. and Mrs. Linder." (I do not remember the details.) "And by the year so and so, a black-haired little boy was marching happily to school in such and such district of Paris." It was much better than this, but that was the method. All I remember today is one sentence—an impressive description characterizing the overall screen image of Linder: "This elegant figure shivering on the screens of the whole world." Old

[1]For an English translation of this pamphlet, see Ayn Rand, *Russian Writings on Hollywood*, edited by Michael S. Berliner (Marina del Rey, CA: Ayn Rand Institute Press, 1999).

movies did shiver, and this comedian was an elegant top-hat-and-cane type. From this one image I realized what colorful writing was. The author could have said, "He is an elegant screen comedian." Instead, he integrated the whole thought into an immediate visual image: an elegant figure shivering on the screens of the whole world. That taught me an important lesson.

The important part of the story is that although I grasped the principle, I could not write that way immediately. I did jazz up my Pola Negri pamphlet a bit: I avoided saying everything in the manner of a direct synopsis. Instead, I came at it a bit indirectly and, when possible, even elaborated from my own imagination. The editor was satisfied, and it was published. But it was not nearly as good as the Max Linder pamphlet.

Until I began writing *We the Living* (in the early thirties), the Max Linder pamphlet remained in my mind as the goal. I thought that this is what an accomplished writer should do, but I also knew that I could not yet do it. But by the time I began writing *We the Living*, I suddenly thought, "Why, I am doing it!" Not consistently, but once in a while. By the time I got to *Atlas Shrugged*, I could almost do it to order.

Developing style involves conditioning your subconscious (which takes years) and, above all, never forcing yourself. I had to wait until I had enough observations and colorful ideas in my subconscious so that the standing orders I gave it could take effect. Only experience will do this, in conjunction with that relaxed permission to your own subconscious to integrate things when and as it can. So do not start aiming at color immediately.

The first thing to remember about style is to forget it. Let it come naturally. You acquire style by practicing. First learn to express your ideas clearly on paper; only then will you notice one day that you are writing in your *own* style. But do not look at the calendar waiting for that day. When you write, focus only on your subject and the clarity with which you present it.

There *are* principles that may help you with style, but this long preface was necessary, because I want to stress that you must not memorize everything I am going to say, nor think about it while you are writing.

In every aspect of style, the absolute standard is your subject and theme. They must determine not only the content and the details, but also the particular words and sentences you select to express them. When you write, do not think about how beautiful your words are, or how people will react, or above all, what it supposedly proves about you. Think exclusively of what you want to say. To the extent to which you can focus on your subject, you will write as best you can at your present stage of development.

It is often said that an artist is selfless—that when he paints or writes, he forgets himself and reality, and sees only his work. The same is said of nonfiction writers. Of course, this is a misapplication of terms, because it means that you have no selfish interest in focusing on your subject—that only being unselfish makes you forget all other considerations but your work. Actually, this exclusive focus on your work is the most selfish thing you can do (in the Objectivist sense of "selfish"[2]), and you ought to train yourself to do it. If you want to write a good article, it is in your interest to do so. But it is a complicated task, which requires the use of your subconscious; you must forget all your other concerns and remember only what you are writing about.

It would not occur to a scientist to focus partly on his experiment and partly on his self-esteem or future fame. (If it does, he is a neurotic and will probably not be heard from.) He has to focus exclusively on his experiment; nothing else is relevant. The same applies to writing, only it is harder because it is a purely mental job—there is nothing in reality yet except a blank sheet of paper. This is why so many people fail at it. It is harder to focus on the reality of what you have to produce when there is nothing before you but a blank page. You have to originate the subject and theme along with everything that goes into carrying out your intention. In practice, therefore, you must be more reality-oriented than a scientist, who has the help of the physical problem and the physical objects he is working with. Aim at being *at least* as reality-oriented as a scientist—which in this context means being *exclusively* focused on your subject.

[2]See *The Virtue of Selfishness*, and especially the introduction and the initial essay, "The Objectivist Ethics."

Focusing on reality means pursuing clarity. The first concern of style is clarity. Remember that approximations will not do. They can occur in your first draft, but they are the first thing to look for in editing. Holding clarity as an absolute is the surest road first to a competent style, and perhaps eventually to a brilliant style of your own.

As I said in "Basic Principles of Literature,"[3] the two main aspects of style—which apply to nonfiction too—are choice of content and choice of words. The first refers to the abstractions or details you choose in order to present a given subject; the second, to the words and sentence structure you choose.

In nonfiction, perhaps the main issue in regard to choice of content is the choice between abstract discourse and concretization. Nonfiction is primarily abstract discourse. It is a presentation of certain views, which means certain principles, which means abstractions. When you write nonfiction, you are communicating knowledge. You are dealing with abstract issues, which you present by means of abstractions, i.e., words and sentences. However, you must remember that only concretes exist—that abstractions are merely a method of classifying concretes. Therefore, if you are writing an abstract essay, the question will necessarily arise: how and when do you tie what you are saying to reality?

To present an abstract principle, you need illustrations. Giving examples (particularly if you are presenting a new theory) ties abstractions to reality—it shows what kinds of concretes illustrate the abstraction you are writing about. This is one form of concretization. But what you do in regard to style is more complex. The color, the metaphors, the unusual verbal gimmicks all involve concretization.

In a nonfiction article, you bring in concretizations or colorful details as a means of integrating your subject in the reader's mind. Specifically, this helps integrate not only the abstraction you are presenting and the concretes to which it applies in reality, but also mind and emotions. Colorful touches achieve the integration to values. This is what I call "good slanted writing." By "slanted," I mean writing which is selective—i.e., ruled by your values—not slanted in

---

[3]*The Romantic Manifesto.*

the sense of distorting reality. In this way you influence not only the mind of the reader, but also his emotions. You appeal to his values.

This sort of concretization is a kind of bridge between nonfiction and fiction writing. The same principle applies to fiction, only in a much more complex way. In choosing value-oriented concretes, you are acting on the fiction-writing premise. Strictly speaking, nonfiction writing is concerned only with clarity of presentation. When you introduce colorful touches, you do so on the same principle by which a fiction writer writes his whole story. You are, in a limited way, borrowing a certain technique from fiction writing.

To illustrate how this works, I am going to analyze my "Brief Comments" on Apollo 8. I want to show you, from the aspect of style, what considerations made me concretize certain points, and what would happen had I written it differently.

The article starts with a paragraph and a half that is strictly informative, nonfiction writing:

The flight of Apollo 8 was a magnificent technological achievement. Leaving aside the question of whether the government should have a space program (which, apart from military defense purposes, it should not), it was an achievement of human intelligence, of man's rational faculty. The knowledge and the precision required to plan, calculate, and execute that flight was such a feat that no one will claim it was done by instinct, feeling, or "arbitrary social convention."

This is pure abstract discussion.

Here is the last sentence of the second paragraph: "That flight was a declaration spectacularly displayed to the whole world: 'This is what man the *rational* being can do.' " This sentence is a concretization of a definite point. Stylistically, it is drama. I could have said, "The flight was a rational achievement," but I had already said that. Therefore, for the purpose of informing the reader, my coming back to the issue of man the rational being was not necessary. Then why did I do it? Here is where theme and subject determine style. What did I want to say about the Apollo 8 flight? I was not discussing the flight as such, nor the epistemological issue of reason versus emotion. I was focusing on a certain image of man and man's achievement.

Why would people feel enthusiastic if Apollo 8 succeeded? Because of a properly human, "collective" self-esteem—the pride and pleasure of knowing about something that man at his best has done. Therefore the meaning of the whole flight, to the general public, is a certain view of man and the flight's significance for man. Man is the ultimate purpose—the consumer of any achievement of science. That is what I wanted to communicate. But if I said this in the terms I am using now, I would not communicate much. You would understand me intellectually, but I would not make the point real, because it would still be an abstraction. If I said, "Man ought to be rational, and we are happy when he is," those are abstract thoughts. But when I switch the reader's focus to an *image* of man, I concretize something. I introduce something which is still an abstraction (namely, an image of man), but I connect it to reality, as the subject of the piece requires.

Now how could I do this briefly? There were several considerations. Observe the integration. (This is the fiction method.) I wanted the reader to feel that this achievement was great and triumphant. So I say, "That flight was a declaration spectacularly displayed to the whole world." I wanted to mention, but only as an aside, that the whole world was watching. Most of all, I wanted to convey the ringing quality, by connotation, of a manifesto: "*This* is what man, the *rational* being can do!" I switched from an abstraction to something emotional and concrete.

Here is what follows: "Mankind was in desperate need of that reminder. Consider the sewer of degradation which is today's culture, and the images of man that it projects." Now I could have presented the rest of this paragraph in informational, nonfiction terms: "In politics, the dominant trend is statism; in ethics, altruism; in epistemology, irrationalism; in esthetics, blind emotionalism." This says a lot, and does so economically, but in an abstract, nonfiction style; I am merely naming intellectual trends. Observe that what I actually wrote is exactly the same thing, but concretized:

Consider . . . the images of man that [our culture] projects: politically, man the rightless slave of the state [instead of simply saying "statism"]; morally, man the congenital incompetent, to whose needs all life is to be sacrificed [I concretize what altruism is]; epistemologically, man the mindless, an irrational creature run by unknowable urges [this is a concretization]; esthetically, man the howling hippie [this is a journalistic concrete].[4]

This is a method of condensing, and thus reminding the reader of, the meaning of the abstractions covered by a single word (such as "statism," "altruism," "irrationalism"). Since the purpose of the article is to tell the reader what the issue of irrationality versus achievement means to a given image of man, I had to make real, in an emotionally arousing way, what sort of images of man are projected today.

In nonfiction terms, I could have concluded this paragraph with: "Therefore the world watched the flight eagerly. It wanted to see a rational achievement." This is a good sentence, which says something important, but it is good enough for a first draft only. What I write in the article is: "If you consider it, you will see that the special intensity, the eagerness, the enthusiasm, with which the world watched the astronauts' journey, came from mankind's hunger for a reassertion of its trampled self-esteem, for a sight of man the hero." This is concretized, even though abstract. (Mankind's self-esteem, for instance, is a huge abstraction.) But it is enough to appeal to the emotions and values in the reader. "Mankind's trampled self-esteem" is a strong metaphor, and the rational reader should feel a certain shudder of indignation at this point—not because I assert it arbitrarily, but because I here prepared the ground for it. I listed how man is predominantly seen today, which confirms the trampling of mankind's self-esteem; I provided the concretes, so when I use such a strong expression I do not do so arbitrarily. And by the time I say "man the hero" (after "man the incompetent" and "man the hippie"), it has an inspiring quality. That is good nonfiction writing, which borrows the methods of fiction.

The next (one-line) paragraph reads: "It is an outrage and a

---

[4]Material in brackets, except for the first, is Ayn Rand's.

tragedy that that sight was undercut." That is an assertion, and merely another attention-arrester. I continue:

> When, from the distance of the moon, from the height of the triumph of science, we expected to hear the astronauts' message and heard, instead, a voice reciting the moldy nonsense which even a slum-corner evangelist would not have chosen as a text—reciting the Bible's cosmology—I, for one, felt as if the capsule had disintegrated and we were left in the primordial darkness of empty space.

At first ("from the distance of the moon," etc.) this is merely selective but factual nonfiction writing. I then write, "the moldy nonsense which even a slum-corner evangelist would not have chosen," in order to concretize my point. I want to invoke, as economically as possible, the questionability of reading the Bible's cosmology. I want the reader to associate it with the place where it belongs, which (in the twentieth century, at least) is below a street-corner evangelist. Next, instead of drawing some abstract conclusion, I describe my personal emotions. This approach is determined by my theme. This is not an article on the importance of reason versus faith; it is a comment on a given event. Therefore, the Objectivist context—namely, the importance of reason—is taken for granted. I do not prove it or propagandize for it, but take it as an absolute. So it would have been inappropriate at this point to talk about the impropriety of mixing faith and science.

My aim was to communicate the importance, and the disastrous effect, of Bible-reading in the context of the triumph of science. To do this, I did not have to explain that Bible-reading is irrational. I had to describe an emotional response, and the strongest I could think of was the one I experienced. But saying, "I, for one, felt sick" or "I felt indignant" would be arbitrary and would fall flat. So I indicate, in concrete terms, *why* I felt that way: because we were back in the darkness of primordial space and the capsule had disintegrated. This is metaphorical in the sense that the capsule was still there. But if we had been looking at Apollo 8 as a great achievement, and then this rational being started reading the Bible, then, from the point of view of the meaning of the event, the capsule *had* disappeared. The value of the intellectual triumph was negated by somebody reciting moldy stuff that nobody takes seriously.

That is what a line and a half accomplished.

The astronauts reading the Bible from space is the subject of my article. The theme is what I think of that act—why it was wrong. So the climax is the paragraph about the Bible-reading. From then on, I am just cashing in on what I have established.

The next paragraph is essentially nonfiction in style:

If you wonder what perpetuates the reign of irrationality on Earth, you have seen a demonstration: it is not done by the worst among men, but by the best—not by the masses of the ignorant, but by the leaders who default on the responsibility of thought—not by witch doctors, but by scientists.

For the most part, this is a straight nonfiction presentation. The point does not call for concretization or an appeal to emotions. The only concretization is "not by witch doctors, but by scientists." This is appropriate in order to concretize the issue of irrationality versus reason. Everybody knows that a witch doctor is the symbol of savagery; and what a scientist is has been demonstrated by the whole article up to that point. Therefore, the juxtaposition of the two concretes adds reality to the nonfiction style of the rest of the paragraph.

The next three paragraphs are a further cashing-in, and were not obligatory. I could have stopped the article with "not by witch doctors, but by scientists." However, I wanted to make a wider point using the same concretes: "No witch doctor's power to encourage mankind's darkest superstitions is comparable to the power of an astronaut broadcasting from the moon."

The next paragraph is a concretization appropriate to the event. It is a conclusion that is pure propaganda, in the good sense of the word. I remind people of what they should have asked themselves long ago about the difference between science and the humanities: "There are two questions that should be asked: Would the astronauts treat the slightest malfunction of the least significant instrument aboard the spacecraft as carelessly and thoughtlessly as they treated the most important issues of philosophy?" You could make the same point by saying that nobody makes airplanes or automobiles as carelessly as they espouse bad philosophy. But when you think of how much depends on the scientific precision of a space flight, then it is irresistible to use this example to point out to people that they do not treat matter as carelessly and thoughtlessly as they treat their own souls. Here is the second question: "And, if not, does not man's spirit deserve the same disciplined, conscientious, *rational* attention that they gave to inanimate matter?"

The final paragraph is pure abstraction: "The flight of Apollo 8 was a condensed dramatization of mankind's tragedy: a demonstration of man's epistemological double standard in the field of science and of the humanities." Putting in such touches of philosophy is not something I recommend to beginners, because it is very difficult to do. Do not attempt it until you are more at home with philosophy on the one hand, and with the subject of your article on the other. It is optional in any case. Since I could do it in three lines, it was appropriate. I included it as a lead for the reader; so much nonsense has been written on the dichotomy between science and the humanities, and I had all the material necessary to indicate what is wrong with this false dichotomy. But it is strictly a reminder to my philosophical readers, for whom it is a valuable springboard to future thinking.

What I mean by dramatizing or concretizing should now be clear. There is no rule about when or how often to concretize; in general, do it when you need to tie a certain aspect of your abstract presentation to reality. Do it to appeal to the reader's emotions (specifically, his sense of value) in an economical way, and to remind him of what specifically is entailed in your presentation.

You need to be careful in judging when this is appropriate. Generally, if you are writing a theoretical article, then stylistically you should include concretizing touches as little as possible. They may be advisable, occasionally, when they grow out of your material, but not as a rule. You do give examples, of course, which is an issue of content. But stylistically, you do not need metaphors or color, because they would detract from the clarity of your presentation.

If you think I am a colorful writer, read *Introduction to Objectivist*

Epistemology. There, I do not permit myself any color (except at the conclusion of each chapter, where I tie the material to its cultural influence or consequences). The book is a strict presentation of theory in almost exclusively literal terms: no metaphors, no jazz—only clarity. However, when you write middle-range articles—when you apply abstractions to concretes—you can permit yourself certain elements of color, if they grow out of your material and you do not force anything. Even then, you must not overdo it. In any nonfiction piece, abstract narrative should predominate. You would not write a theoretical article consisting of nothing but examples, and the same applies to these stylistic, concretizing touches. They should be few, and used only when you have a reason for them, not to display your virtuosity or show off your imagination.

Now let me add that these concretizations or dramatic touches are not the only elements of style. Straight narrative itself—the most abstract nonfiction writing—has an element of style, too. It too involves a characteristic, distinctive manner of expression. The driest presentation of even an outline or high school synopsis still contains elements of your particular form of expression, because how you communicate always comes from your individual psycho-epistemology. Since no two of these are exactly alike, everything you write has a certain element of individual style. In the case of a dry synopsis, the variation in the styles of different individuals is minimal; in the case of narrative passages, there are major differences.

To sum up: one of the chief factors distinguishing individual style is when, how, and to what extent a writer concretizes.

The other main subdivision of style is word-choice.

There cannot be a rule that only one choice of words will communicate a given thought. I said earlier that you should not aim at the "perfect" article, because it does not exist. Similarly, do not aim at some "perfect" words for a given thought, if only you could get them. They do not exist. The possibilities are limitless, and there are many options. Clarity and precision are the only absolutes. So be guided by the choice of words that expresses your thought as clearly and precisely as possible.

Concretization or emotional appeal enters the issue of word-choice in the form of the connotation of words.

Clarity depends exclusively on the *denotation*—the exact meaning—of words. But given a particular thought that you want to express, the specific words you use can make a great difference, because in any language there are subtle distinctions of meaning among certain words. Those distinctions determine the *connotations* of your words; by means of these connotations you achieve the same purpose that you gain by touches of concretization in the choice of content.

For example, if you describe a woman as slender, the connotation is entirely different than if you describe her as lanky. While there is a little more than connotation involved here, the words "slender" and "lanky" both describe people who are thin. But the former connotes someone graceful and beautiful; the latter, someone gawky and awkward. Almost every adjective has a series of semi-synonyms of this kind, and you need to be careful about which one you select.

I remember a short story in which the author, describing a hero, wrote: "He looked well scrubbed." She wanted to convey that he was clean-cut, in the serious, intellectual sense. But when you say "well scrubbed," the immediate connotation is non-intellectual; it suggests someone who spends a lot of time in the bathroom with soap and water. By evoking that image, she achieved an unintended effect. That is what you should watch out for. (Most people choose words almost "instinctively"; this choice is so automatized that, usually, a person simply knows when he has chosen the wrong word.)

Watch out for philosophical implications, too. For example, if someone writes, "He had an instinct for courage," he may only want to convey, "He is brave." But the actual, and improper, implication is that courage is an instinct.

You must also watch out for the cultural corruption of words. No word can be inherently controversial, but it can become so by protracted cultural usage. For example, today, if you say that somebody is idealistic, it has the connotation of impractical foolishness. Strictly speaking, the word does not mean that. But if you know the word is used that way, do not use it unless your context makes clear what *you* mean by it.

It is important to know when to continue using a word despite its being corrupted, and when to drop such a word. The real test is:

what does the corruption of the word accomplish? For example, I fight for the word "selfishness,"[5] even though the word, as used colloquially, designates both criminals and Peter Keatings, on the one hand, and also productive industrialists and Howard Roarks, on the other.[6] Here, there is an attempt to obliterate a legitimate concept—selfishness—and thus we should not give up the word. (The same is true for "capitalism.")

By contrast, take the word "liberal." In the nineteenth century, this was a proper term which stood for one who defended rights and limited government—except that it never represented a fully consistent political philosophy. So historically, what started as nineteenth-century liberalism gradually became modern liberalism. (Conservatives used to claim they were the true liberals, but they have given up doing so.) Similarly, some people today use "libertarian" to designate the pro–free enterprise position, but there are some modern liberals who call themselves libertarian as well. This stealing of terms with undefined connotations is so prevalent today that I simply do not use any of these words. This is *one* reason I prefer "pro-capitalist" to "conservative." When what is being disguised or destroyed is not exactly what you uphold, then drop the word and use another.

As a rule, the right connotations contribute to clarity. In other words, there is no necessary conflict between the exact denotation of a word, and its particular shading or emotional connotation. Sometimes, however, the two do conflict: a certain word appeals to you because it has the right emotional connotation, but it does not express what you want to say as clearly as another, less emotional, word. In such cases, sacrifice emotional connotation. I have thrown out beautiful passages I loved, because I found, in editing, that they clashed with clarity. If it is a clash between color and clarity, then the color goes. Of course, ultimately the writing then is much *more* colorful, because the color grows out of, and supports, the material.

[5]See the introduction to *The Virtue of Selfishness*.
[6]Peter Keating and Howard Roark, both architects, are characters from *The Fountainhead*. Peter Keating is a dependent, conformist parasite. Howard Roark is the hero—a first-hander, an innovator, and an egoist.

I will speak briefly about metaphors. Metaphors, which are comparisons of one thing to another, should manipulate properly the consciousness of your reader. For instance, if you say, "The snow was white as sugar," it gives you an impression of that snow. It makes it concrete—and thus much clearer and more real—than if you had said, "The snow was white." Saying that "The sugar was white as snow" does the same thing. The principle is that a metaphor isolates the particular attribute of a given sensory image in order to make the reader fully aware of it. "The snow was white" and "The sugar was white" are merely abstractions. But if you say, "The snow was white as sugar," you make the reader hold in his mind, for a split second, the two concrete images. He has an image of sugar and one of snow, and he sees what they have in common. It is like reconstructing the process of concept-formation in his mind—of observing what attributes two concretes have in common.

Whenever you read a passage which contains a metaphor you like, monitor what it actually does for you. You will see that, in an automatized way, the metaphor concretizes a given attribute of a sight or event or situation, thus making it real to you.

That is all there is to the issue of metaphors. I make this point because the greatest mystery is made of this subject in literary courses, particularly in English departments.

So much, in a general way, about the positive side of developing a style. On the negative side, there are several "don'ts," i.e., practices, that I strongly suggest you avoid.

Don't #1: Don't say something in a complicated manner when it can be said simply. Sometimes this error is caused by a mistake in thinking, when a writer has not thought something through adequately and therefore cannot say what he wants in a simple manner. But I am speaking strictly about style here, where a writer does understand the content of his passage clearly, but nevertheless puts words together in a complicated way.

Some writers do this deliberately to conceal the fact that they have nothing to say. Nietzsche has a line [in *Thus Spake Zarathustra*] about poets muddying their waters to make them appear deep. Other writers do it so that people will not understand too clearly what they are saying. The archetype here is Immanuel Kant. Most of today's newspaper and magazine reporting is a combination of the "muddied waters" approach and a gutter version of Kant. Its authors write so vaguely that they hide the fact that (1) they have nothing much to say, and (2) what they have to say is so evil that no one would accept it if they said it straight. That is predominantly the way liberals write; they use every euphemism and indirection possible in order not to say that they are advocating dictatorship.

I want to focus here on stylistic errors, however, not on the intention to hide or disguise something.

As an editor, I often correct sentences which, for example, use five words where two would do. That is a purely grammatical issue. In this respect, it is good practice to assume that you have been given an assignment of a certain number of words. You would be surprised what economy this teaches. In fact, you should write this way even if you have 700,000 words to use, as I did in *Atlas Shrugged*. That novel is very economically written given what it says. I was sharply aware of trying not to use a word or a thought that did not contribute something important. Therefore, whether it is a newspaper column or a long novel, the principle is the same: write economically. In editing, try to see how many sentences can be simplified. See if fewer words will convey the same meaning.

Consider this example of one very abused structure: "It is this issue that contributed to the destruction of the culture." A simpler way of stating this is: "This issue contributed to the destruction of the culture." There are contexts in which the more complex form is necessary, because it has a different emphasis—for example, as a conclusion to a certain development. But I often encounter that structure where it is unnecessary, and then it is very awkward.

Here is another example: "Because A, B, and C—D will result." Do not start a long sentence with the word "because." The reader does not know at the start that you are talking about D, and so you make him retain too many subsidiary or conditional clauses without his knowing why. Do not overload your reader's mind. You *are* entitled to assume that he is conscientious—that he is not skimming quickly to the bottom of your paragraph, but is going at an even pace and is trying to grasp every word and sub-clause as you present it. But if you use a "because" in this way, your reader may have to return to the beginning of the sentence and reread it.

Every rule of this kind has exceptions. In fact, stylistic rules are made to be broken. If you observe them properly, you can sometimes achieve great effects by deliberately breaking them. For example, in one scene in *We the Living*, there is a sentence which runs for almost an entire page, in which I use a lot of subsidiary "because's" separated by colons. It was a deliberate fiction device—a montage of dramatic concretes before I came to the conclusion which followed from these concretes: "—Leo Kovalensky was sentenced to die."

Don't #2: Don't use a "seventy-five-cent word" where a two-syllable word will do. Memorizing the more obscure parts of the dictionary is not erudition; and erudition (or the desire to show it) is not part of style. The simpler the words, the better.

I do not have in mind a folksy, artificial way of talking down to the reader, which one finds in today's political literature. When I say "use simple words," I mean it in the best sense. The simplest words in a language are the most expressive. So question the meaning of anything you cannot convey in simple words. Of course, a word like "epistemology" is not simple (though it is so in the basic vocabulary of philosophy). You need not avoid words for which there are no synonyms. But to use an example I got from Leonard Peikoff: if you want to say, "He said stubbornly," do not use, "He asseverated contumaciously."

The archvillain here is William Buckley, who makes a clown of himself. His trademark is to use words he probably spends half his time looking up in the dictionary. He expects you not to know them, and therefore to feel guilty and inferior. But the real effect is that you lose interest.

Whenever you feel the need to use a word like "contumaciously," do not. There are plenty of simple synonyms which are more expressive and direct. Whenever your reader fails to understand a word, you destroy the effect of the content on him. Yet the main purpose of style is to communicate content as clearly and powerfully as possible.

As to the origins of such words, some are obsolete, while others come from obscure, erudite sources à la Kant. They might have been used by writers who wanted to appear to be scholars rather than "common men." They are predominantly archaic, academic remnants; no good writer today uses them. For instance, a good nonfiction writer (whose ideas are atrocious) is Erich Fromm. He writes in simple terms which are valid both for his colleagues and for educated laymen. He is the opposite of Buckley in that respect. This, incidentally, contributes to Fromm's prominence.

Don't #3: Don't use pejorative adjectives, sarcasm, or inappropriate humor.

In a first draft, it is sometimes valuable to express your feelings fully. For example, in a first draft, I have even written "abysmal bastards," knowing this would not go into the final version. I was indicating that I need to project strong indignation and to prove it.

If moral indignation is justified, then why are such words bad, stylistically? Because they are too easy. Unsupported expressions of emotion (e.g., insulting or pejorative adjectives) are arbitrary stylistically, and, philosophically, constitute emotionalism. They have the same stylistic effect as the kind of quarrel which consists of "Says you, says I"; they always weaken an article. Even if you give reasons for your strong language, understatement is usually more desirable.

When you understate something, the reader is aware of what you are saying; his own mind then supplies the rest, which is what you want. But when you overstate something, you deafen the reader. You do not give him time to come to his own conclusion. It is as if you were shouting at him. Observe that on stage—while there are situations in which nothing can substitute for a scream—in most of the famous dramatic scenes, it is the whispered, simple sentence that gives you chills. When you overstate something, you disarm yourself. A man does not shout when he is sure of his case. When a writer understates what he is saying, what comes across is an overwhelming assurance on his part.

At one point in my article "Requiem for Man,"[7] on the anti-

---

[7]*Capitalism: The Unknown Ideal.*

capitalist papal encyclical *Populorum Progressio* ("On the Development of Peoples"), I felt like referring to the Pope as "the abysmal bastard" or worse, because I felt almost unbearable indignation. Instead, I communicated what I thought by understatement: "Anyone who evades that image [i.e., of life under the system advocated by the encyclical] . . . and declares that human effort is not a sufficient reason for a man to keep his own product—may claim any motive but love of humanity." There are circumstances in which it is proper to use a blatantly pejorative adjective, but they are the exceptions.

The same point applies to sarcasm, which should be used sparingly. The general principle is to prepare the ground for what you want to treat sarcastically. Make sure it is clear why you are making a sarcastic remark. Without that context, sarcasm amounts stylistically to the argument from intimidation:[8] you "persuade" the reader through intimidation, saying, in effect, "I will not take you seriously if you say A, and I dismiss it sarcastically." But in and of itself, it is of no consequence that you, the author, dismiss something. When you have prepared your ground, however, a touch of sarcasm can be stylistically brilliant.

There are some subjects which one can discuss only sarcastically, e.g., the hippies or modern art. There the *subject* gives you the necessary ground. It is a caricature in itself, and therefore you cannot evaluate it except in sarcastic terms (though you *can* discuss its psychological and philosophical roots seriously). For instance, in my article "The 'Inexplicable Personal Alchemy,' " when I move from the Russian rebels to the American rebels, I am sarcastic from the outset. I write: "America, too, has a vanguard of young rebels, dissenters, and fighters for freedom. Marching down the aisle of a theater, they shout their protest to the world: 'I cannot travel without a passport! . . . I am not allowed to smoke marijuana! . . . I am not allowed to take my clothes off!' " I say that the hippies are "puppets in search of a master" and "exhibitionists who have nothing to exhibit," etc., which are sarcastic metaphors. Yet there was no other way to describe them.

What I say about sarcasm applies to any kind of humor. Humor

---

[8]See Ayn Rand, "The Argument from Intimidation," in *The Virtue of Selfishness.*

must be justified by your content. If you have not let the reader in on what you are laughing at and why, then humor is inappropriate. It becomes a substitute for giving a reason—again, a form of the argument from intimidation; instead of refuting a position, you dismiss it with humor.

There are two broad categories of tone: serious and humorous. Which approach you take depends on your evaluation of your subject—on whether you want to treat it seriously or make fun of it. As a general principle, a theoretical article must be serious. You *might* include touches of humor, but only as exceptions. As a basic approach, it would be extremely inappropriate to write a theoretical article in a humorous tone, because you would be laughing at your own material. It is only the middle-range article that offers a wider choice here.

In essence, humor is the denial of the importance or metaphysical validity of something. Therefore, the type of humor you use depends on what you are laughing at. If you laugh at something evil, your humor will have a benevolent quality. If you laugh at the good, it will have a malicious quality.

When I say it is proper to laugh at evil, I do not mean all evil. It is improper, under all circumstances, to write humorously about tragic and painful events or issues—about death, cemeteries, torture chambers, concentration camps, executions, etc. This is called "sick humor," and the designation is correct, because although it is possible to laugh at such things, one should not consider them funny. For example, take comedies about the Nazis. I have a strong aversion to war comedies. War *per se* is bad enough, but war and dictatorship combined are *a fortiori* not a subject for comedy. This applies to fiction and nonfiction writing.

Just as you should not treat tragic or painful evil humorously, neither should you treat an important, good subject humorously. If, for example, with the best intentions in the world, you wrote humorously about the heroic element in man, it would not be a good article—the issue is metaphysically important. Usually, if someone makes fun of heroes, it is not because he wants to glorify them, but because he is against heroism.

As an example of appropriate humor in a nonfiction article, take

the passage on Hegel in the title essay of *For the New Intellectual.*[9]
Describing Hegel's philosophy, I write that "omniscience about the
physical universe . . . is to be derived, not from observations of the
facts, but from the contemplation of [the] Idea's triple somersaults
inside his, Hegel's, mind." The reference to triple somersaults is
meant to be light or humorous. I am not denying the seriousness of
the subject (the history of philosophy), but I am indicating that I do
not take Hegel seriously and that we need not worry about this particular monster.

As a general conclusion about humor, observe that appropriate
humor requires a community of basic premises among those whom
you expect to laugh. For instance, if we disapprove of Hegel, and I
make a crack about him, it will be funny to you only because your
basic estimate of him is the same as mine. But it would not be funny
to a Hegelian, and you should keep this in mind. If you write an article intended to persuade religious people that religion is wrong, a
humorous approach would be totally wrong—your readers do not
share your premises, and your humor will fall flat. In writing about
ideas you oppose, use humor only when you know it is based on what
your audience considers funny.

Don't #4: Don't use bromides. Bromides are canned integrations.
They were good the first time they were used, which is why they became bromides. When writing a first draft, if you need some color
and a bromide occurs to you, but you want to continue writing, it is
fine to keep it there as a temporary indication of a thought. But do
not let it stay in your final version.

Bromides defeat themselves. In *The Fountainhead*, Austin Heller
said that all the houses offered to him were so alike, so similar to
what he had seen before, that he could not see them at all. Something too familiar becomes invisible. Similarly, bromides do not add
color—they merely wipe out what you want to stress. If in editing
you cannot find a colorful touch of your own, omit the color and use
straight narrative. Do not leave in bromides. They give an impression of improper imitation.

[9]Ayn Rand, *For the New Intellectual* (New York: New American Library, 1961).

There are, of course, exceptions. For example, if you are discussing someone like Hubert Humphrey and want to show that he is imitative or a windbag, then select from his speeches the most bromidic passages, provided they are not accidental. If a politician speaks well but occasionally uses a bromide, and you select those exceptions, that is dishonest; but if you are characterizing someone like Humphrey, you have a choice of riches, because everything he says is either obfuscation or a bromide.

Don't #5: Do not use unnecessary synonyms. It was commonly held that a writer should never repeat a given word within a certain number of lines. On this view, if you used the same word twice in close proximity, you had to make a change. This is a grave error.

The simplest examples of this error are found in some old novels, where the author wants to indicate that the characters are talking:

"How do you do?" he said.

"Very well, thank you," she answered.

"I'm glad to hear it," he asserted.

"Oh, are you?" she uttered.

The result is an awkward collection of artificial synonyms. If you want to say "he said" and "she said," just say it. Do not look for unnecessary synonyms.

The same error occurs in nonfiction. For instance, if the word "philosophy" comes up too often, you might be tempted to look for synonyms, e.g., "wisdom," "ideology," "body of thought," "world view." Although it *is* awkward to use the same word six times in two sentences, the solution is not to substitute a synonym, but to recast the sentence so as not to need to repeat the word. Often you can simply use a pronoun, e.g., "it" instead of "philosophy." But if the repetition of the word is necessary, and reconstructing the sentence leads to unnecessary complications, then simply repeat the word. This will not jump out at the reader if the context requires it.

It is better to repeat a word, even if doing so is slightly obtrusive, than to substitute an unnatural synonym for the sake of form alone. When you use a synonym, not because you need a different shade of meaning, but strictly to avoid repetition, the result sounds phony. Moreover, when you change words not for content but for form, the reader gets the impression that you are changing the subject, and the result is confusing. This is particularly true in philosophy, where there are no exact synonyms. For example, "philosophy" does not have quite the same meaning as "world view" or "body of thought." In fact, there are few literal synonyms for any word. A thesaurus usually provides words with not quite identical meanings. In a nonfiction work, particularly on a serious subject, any time you change a word you introduce a slightly different connotation, and the reader will be justified in thinking that you are talking about something else.

I want to turn now to some problem areas in the realm of style: emphasis, transitions, rhythm, and drama.

Emphasis

Sometimes a sentence is awkward, but you cannot figure out why. The principle here is the same as in the rest of writing: when in doubt, refer to your exact meaning. Just as in your article as a whole you refer to your theme as your standard, so in any particular sentence that seems awkward, refer to what precisely you want to say.

The variety of grammatical structures possible in English permits you to put the emphasis where you want it. The same words combined into a grammatical sentence will yield a different emphasis depending on how you arrange them. Therefore, if you have corrected any obvious problems and a sentence still seems awkward, your emphasis is probably misplaced. For instance, I once heard a beautiful line of poetry that went something like this: "Because you smiled at me, I was happy all day." If it was: "I was happy all day because you smiled at me," its emphasis, and thus its meaning, would be different. (Both arrangements are grammatically permissible.) In the line from the poem, the emphasis is on the fact that the speaker's happiness is owed to the smile of his beloved. In the other version, the emphasis is on his happiness; the cause is incidental.

In an article once in *Esquire*, a number of people (myself included) were asked what the Apollo 11 astronauts should say when they land on the moon. One comedienne suggested: "Miami Beach, it isn't."[10] Now if you said, "It isn't Miami Beach," the meaning would be different. It is not simply the somewhat Yiddish word structure, but the misplaced emphasis. In the form the comedienne used, the thought is on Miami Beach—that is what she expects, and her first reaction is: "Well, it isn't Miami Beach." Therefore, she is not interested. But the other version—"It isn't Miami Beach"—has no particular meaning, because it also isn't New York and it isn't Paris; so it does not communicate the same thought that was achieved by that odd construction.

For examples of this kind of manipulation of emphasis by means of word placement, read *Time* magazine. For instance, I remember *Time* describing some ambitious, energetic man with the words: "No slouch, he." This is typical of the magazine. The practice is not fully permissible grammatically, though it is clear and achieves a certain emphasis. If you wrote, "He is no slouch," it would not be as strong. Incidentally, although the style is amusing, *Time* ruins it by using it constantly. Once you become accustomed to a distortion, it is simply a distortion and it loses emphasis. So use this sort of trick sparingly.

Finally, note that whenever there are several grammatically permissible alternatives, the smoothest will be the one that carries your exact emphasis.

Transitions

There is a great deal of misunderstanding about transitions. Some believe you should always indicate a transition from paragraph to paragraph—but in fact you could not make a worse mistake. If it were true, you would also need a transition from sentence to sentence—but then what would be the transition from a sentence to a transition? Transitions are not necessary if your sentences follow one

[10]William H. Honan, "Le Mot Juste for the Moon," *Esquire*, July 1969. The comedienne is Yetta Bronstein (1968 "Jewish Mother" candidate for President). Ayn Rand's own response was: "What hath man wrought!"

another *logically*. Logic is the link between sentences, paragraphs, chapters, and volumes.

When discussing a certain aspect of your subject, if you proceed to the next paragraph and are still discussing that aspect, that is a logical transition and no special bridge is necessary. A transition is needed only when you switch to a different aspect of your subject. If its connection to the immediate discussion is not clear, you need a transition. But if in a certain discussion each sentence follows from the preceding one, and each paragraph follows from the preceding one, then you can rely on your reader's own power of integration. You must assume your reader can hold a progression in mind. If your presentation is clear and logical, but your reader cannot keep in mind what you were discussing in paragraph #1, and why #2 and #3 follow, then he cannot read the article anyway, and no transition would help. Do not write on the premise that you must lead the reader by the hand every time you move to a new paragraph.

A paragraph serves the same function as a period. It is a pause, which unobtrusively makes the reader realize that he is coming to the end of something and that the author is starting on some new, though connected, development. The reader has to integrate this quickly and automatically.

As you edit your article, be the reader's guide. If you introduce a certain idea and in the next five paragraphs discuss various aspects of it, then, when you begin the next sequence, you should perhaps remind your reader of your main idea. (This is not really a transition, but a reminder.) Judge whether a progression is too long for the reader to keep in mind. But aside from these reminders, provide transitions only when there is a specific change of direction or aspect for which the reader cannot immediately see the need.

In fiction writing, transitions must be hidden. But in nonfiction, the more openly and simply you indicate a (necessary) transition, the better, because hidden transitions here are confusing and artificial. For example, suppose you were talking about the politics of a mixed economy and now want to discuss economics. Simply say: "Now let us consider the economics of a mixed economy," or: "Turning to economics." Take the reader into your confidence. If your

THE ART OF NONFICTION

indication is brief and logical, he will know automatically that you are changing aspects, and he will integrate them.

If you fail to include a necessary transition, your reader will begin the new paragraph, pause, read the next sentence, and then return to the preceding paragraph to establish the transition himself. In effect, he thinks: "Oh, I see. He is now discussing economics instead of politics." Never force your reader to do that.

The simplest and most open transition is best. But suppose you say: "Now that we have discussed the politics of a mixed economy, we will next turn to the economics of a mixed economy." This kind of repetition is annoying, unnecessary, and confusing. The reader operates on the assumption that everything the author does is for a purpose. If you offer the reader unnecessary recapitulations, he will ask himself what he missed—why this purposeful writer finds it necessary to repeat something. The result is that you momentarily lose the reader.

It is sometimes necessary to number the subdivisions of an issue. For instance, if you are discussing the bad consequences of a mixed economy and want to make sure your reader remembers them all, then number each of the consequences. If you use this method occasionally, it will help to integrate your material. The numbers remind the reader that these points are all part of one development. And if it is a lengthy discussion, by the time the reader finishes with consequence #5, he can easily refer back to the beginning of the sequence and remind himself of the others. But do not abuse this method. If at several places you use a sentence followed by a series of numbers, it becomes too hard to follow.

When you use the numerical method, be sure to indicate clearly when you are beyond your numbered points. Often the content will do this, but sometimes you need a transitional sentence to indicate that you have finished with consequence #5 and are proceeding to the next development. There are many ways of doing it, but the simplest form of this transition is something like: "Such are the consequences of a mixed economy."

Sometimes the sentence structure itself provides a transition from one development to another. Since this is a complex method,

I want to illustrate it from my article "What is Romanticism?" Here are the first two paragraphs:

> Romanticism is a category of art based on the recognition of the principle that man possesses the faculty of volition.
>
> Art is a selective re-creation of reality according to an artist's metaphysical value-judgments. An artist recreates those aspects of reality which represent his fundamental view of man and of existence. In forming a view of man's nature, a fundamental question one must answer is whether man possesses the faculty of volition—because one's conclusions and evaluations in regard to all the characteristics, requirements and actions of man depend on the answer.

First, I give a generalized definition of Romanticism. (Of course, I will have to validate that definition.) Moving to a wider abstraction, I next define art. I indicate how an artist presents his fundamental view of man and of existence, and that with respect to man, a fundamental question is whether or not he possesses volition.

This abstract information lays the foundation for what follows. But I must return to how this affects the nature of Romanticism. Here is my next sentence (the third paragraph): "Their opposite answers to this question constitute the respective basic premises of two broad categories of art: Romanticism, which recognizes the existence of man's volition—and Naturalism, which denies it." The sentence structure provides the transition, which is in the first part of this sentence.

Observe that I could have omitted this transition and begun the third paragraph with: "There are two broad categories of art," etc. That would be clear, but there would still be a slight jump. So instead I make a verbal bridge, which I include in the sentence structure in place of a separate transition. Instead of declaring, "There are two categories," I say, "Their opposite answers to this question"—I have not yet said who "they" are—"constitute the respective basic premises of two broad categories of art," and then I name them. In this way I form a transition from the generalized abstract discussion, which merely indicated the foundation, to the specific subject of the article. I make the transition to the discussion of Romanticism by tying it verbally, within the same sentence, to the preceding development. That makes for smoother reading. It forms a connection in the reader's mind, and it indicates why I provided the abstract foundation. It also indicates why I divide art into these two broad categories and what their essentials are. Before I go into any further discussion of the two categories, I indicate that they have opposite answers to a question which is fundamental to any art. Thus, I kill several birds with one sentence.

I call this a sentence-structure transition, in that I do not use a separate statement to indicate that I am going from the abstract to the concrete subject of this article.

It would be awkward, however, to start an article that way. If "Their opposite answers," etc. were the first sentence, a series of unanswered questions would immediately arise: Why am I putting something in reverse? Why do I start without indicating what the fundamental question is? Why do I want to discuss two broad categories before I have named them?

Stylistically, a smooth flowing presentation depends especially on the inner logic of the progression of thought. If you follow this logic and do not pause too much between sentences, the result (after some editing) will be a smooth, logically connected presentation. A presentation which strikes you as awkward or jumpy, by contrast, is the result of a writer's uncertainty. Either he is not following the inner logic himself, or he has not fully integrated the progression of thought even in his own mind. Thus he writes at random, or, more frequently, he tries to write by his conscious mind, sentence by deliberate sentence. (This is one bad consequence of attempting to write by a conscious method, without subconscious integration.)

Rhythm

Rhythm is such a tricky problem area that, in effect, I advise you to leave it alone.

In poetry, the rhythm of a sentence is formalized; when you use one type, you know what category it belongs to, so it is not a problem. But the rhythm of a prose sentence is a complex issue. Rhythm, after all, pertains primarily to the realm of *music*, not concepts. It has to do with the way certain sounds register in our brain. Rhythm is the progression and timing of sounds, and the intervals between them. Therefore, the trouble here is the same as with music: we do not yet have an objective vocabulary of music, and thus we cannot say objectively why a certain combination of sounds affects us in a certain way.[11] At present, it is impossible to define precise principles by which to determine whether or not a given sentence is rhythmical.

Rhythm involves not only psychology, but neurology. It involves the way sensations reach our brain, along with the timing of, and the relationships among, these sensations. This is not a mystical, but a perceptual sense—a sense pertaining to the development of our organ of hearing.

So do not worry about this issue, and do not aim consciously at "good rhythm." Let it come naturally. As you write, you will develop your own sense of rhythm. Whenever you begin to feel you need an extra word or syllable, you are developing a sense of rhythm, and you would do well to observe it. In this issue, as in music, ultimately it is each man for himself. For the time being, you must rely on your own sense of rhythm. Go by whatever your own ear senses as smooth or awkward. (There is, however, a lot of agreement about what constitutes a good or bad sentence rhythmically.)

There is a correlation between rhythm and emphasis. Whenever your sentence is wrong in emphasis, chances are it will also be awkward in rhythm. It will sound uneven or unfinished somehow. Similarly, there is a correlation between rhythm and precision. A sentence may also sound uneven if it includes unnecessary words— but this is not a guaranteed correlation.

To give you an example of good and bad rhythm, consider a line from my article "What is Romanticism?" I write: "Man cannot live without philosophy, and neither can he write." I think this is properly rhythmical. But now suppose I had written: "Man cannot live without philosophy, and he cannot write much." The problem is not

[11] See Ayn Rand's discussion of music in "Art and Cognition," *The Romantic Manifesto*.

simply content (though the content is slightly different in each case, which illustrates the connection between rhythm and precision); the sentence is bad rhythmically. It sounds chopped off—as if it had no business ending on that particular syllable.

When we hear sounds, our integrating mechanism requires a certain balance. Musical sequences are usually divided into equivalent phrase groups. The logic of the structure thus requires that the sequence be fulfilled; if it is not, one feels unsatisfied and somewhat agitated. There is a feeling of something incomplete or unbalanced. An unfinished musical phrase is awful, and the same issue is involved in the rhythm of sentences.

Be sure to avoid rhymes. "Poems" without rhymes are neither prose nor poetry—they are nothing. For the same reason, a rhyme in a prose sentence is out of place, and thus distracts your attention by taking your mind to another medium. Moreover, it sounds artificial. If a rhyme occurs in prose, it can create all kinds of confusion.

If you ever have to choose between rhythm and clarity, sacrifice rhythm. Short of that, always adjust bad rhythm, because it is important to a good style. Generally, this is not difficult. The extra word or syllable can usually be found.

When and if someone defines what constitutes rhythm (and this will take a neurologist, a psychologist, and an esthetician), we will have more exact principles to work with. But it is not necessary to be omniscient on this subject. It is appropriate to go by your own sense of rhythm. If you have not developed one, that is not necessarily a writing flaw. So do not worry much about rhythm.

Like everything else about style, rhythm must never be aimed at consciously. More than any other aspect of style, it must come about naturally, by means of subconscious integration.

Drama

In nonfiction, drama is a way of capturing or holding the reader's interest. With rare exceptions, drama belongs not in theoretical, but in middle-range articles. It involves an indirect approach which must be brief and which consists of saying something unexpected or intriguing. It usually involves starting out of context, or uttering something a couple of paragraphs earlier than the logical progression requires.

To give an extreme example, suppose a writer begins an article: "You are a murderer whether you know it or not." That is a dramatic opening, and it is certainly intriguing. It arrests your attention immediately. The author then proceeds to explain that the article is about the welfare state, and that if you ever voted for any welfare measures, you are responsible for an unknown amount of destruction—and maybe even for deaths. He concludes by saying that you are as bad as a murderer if you vote for liberals. The above is an exaggeration, but it illustrates the method by which one achieves drama.

Do not aim at drama consciously (particularly if you are a beginning writer). If you do, the result will be not dramatic but artificial. Let any drama grow out of your material. When you are at home with a straight, logical presentation, then touches of drama might occur to you spontaneously—in which case, they will often be just right and will add a colorful, attention-arresting element to your material. But do not try to force this. Remember, drama is not the essence of nonfiction writing, contrary to what some writing courses teach.

Finally, as in all issues of style, if there is ever a clash between drama and clarity, sacrifice drama.

I want next to compare two different styles. I will present passages from two journalistic articles that treat the same material, and will thereby make the different stylistic elements clear. Observe here the choice of content and the choice of words, and how different basic premises affect the presentations.

Both articles cover the launching of Apollo 11 in 1969, and each passage consists of (1) a description of the crowd in Titusville (the closest town to the launch site, about ten miles away) the night before the launch, and (2) a description of Apollo 11 at night from across the river.

From "Apollo 11" by Ayn Rand[12]

On the shore of the Indian River, we saw cars, trucks, trailers filling every foot of space on both sides of the drive, in the vacant lots, on the lawns, on the river's sloping embankment. There were tents perched at the edge of the water; there were men and children sleeping on the roofs of station wagons, in the twisted positions of exhaustion; I saw a half-naked man asleep in a hammock strung between a car and a tree. These people had come from all over the country to watch the launching across the river, miles away. (We heard later that the same patient, cheerful human flood had spread through all the small communities around Cape Kennedy that night, and that it numbered one million persons.) I could not understand why these people would have such an intense desire to witness just a few brief moments; some hours later I understood it.

It was still dark as we drove along the river. The sky and the water were a solid spread of dark blue that seemed soft, cold, and empty. But, framed by the motionless black leaves of the trees on the embankment, two things marked off the identity of the sky and the earth: far above the sky, there was a single, large star; and on earth, far across the river, two enormous sheaves of white light stood shooting motionlessly into the empty darkness from two tiny upright shafts of crystal that looked liked glowing icicles; they were Apollo 11 and its service tower.

From "Apollo's Great Leap for the Moon" by Loudon Wainwright[13]

All along the shoulders of U.S. Highway #1 and packed solid to the river that ran near it were thousands of trailers, camping vans, tents, makeshift shelters of all kinds. People lolled in the grass, infants were sleeping in cradles on the hoods and tops of cars, fathers and

[12]The Voice of Reason.
[13]Life, vol. 67, no. 4, July 25, 1969.

sons were setting up telescopes, bands of the young in trunks and bikinis ran everywhere. Clearly visible through the night about 10 miles away was the Apollo 11, bathed in searchlights, a tiny stalk of light in the darkness, and this vast picnic crowd had gathered to see the booster belch out its tremendous power, and hurl likenesses of themselves at the Moon.

By morning there were many more—campsites, beaches, jetties, every place of viewing space was jammed with the watchers, and it was extraordinary indeed to drive past miles of faces staring toward 30 seconds of history.

The main point to observe, stylistically, is *showing* versus *telling*.[14] I am not a reporter by profession, but in my article I operated on a premise that reporters do not use today (if they did, they would be giants of journalism)—namely, to be a literal reporter. I *show* you the scene, I do not tell you about it. If you want your readers to feel as if they were there, then concretize the event selectively. Stay away from generalities. I tried to reconstruct the event exactly as I saw it, almost deliberately omitting any editorial interference. I gave my editorial viewpoint by means of concretes; whether the reader accepts it or not, he feels he has seen the event. The typical reporter, however, merely tells you about an event.

Observe how this is done. For instance, I write: "On the shore of the Indian River, we saw cars, trucks, trailers filling every foot of space on both sides of the drive, in the vacant lots, on the lawns, on the river's sloping embankment." Wainwright writes: "All along the shoulders of U.S. Highway #1 and packed solid to the river that ran near it were thousands of trailers, camping vans, tents, makeshift shelters of all kinds." His big mistake stylistically is "of all kinds." It was unnecessary. He lists all the different types of vehicles and where they were placed, as do I. But I tell you they were in every available foot of space and provide some examples of the kinds of space. I give you enough concretes so that you get the impression that it is a large

[14]See the chapters on style in Ayn Rand, *The Art of Fiction: A Guide for Writers and Readers*, edited by Tore Boeckmann (New York: Plume, 2000), and the relevant discussion in "Basic Principles of Literature," *The Romantic Manifesto*.

crowd. I did not make any generalized estimates. It is sufficient to say there were cars, trucks, trailers. The reader can project that those are not the only kinds of vehicles. But when Wainright adds "makeshift shelters of all kinds," that is improper abstraction. It destroys the reality of the concretes, because you cannot, in reality, see such a thing as "of all kinds." He destroys the firsthand perception of the scene, giving the reader instead an editorial summation.

Similarly, he writes that "bands of the young in trunks and bikinis ran everywhere." "Ran everywhere" involves the same mistake. He cannot literally mean everywhere, so it is a sloppy way of saying, "I saw many of them." Such an exaggerated generality destroys the concrete reality of the sight.

His best line is: "it was extraordinary indeed to drive past miles of faces staring toward 30 seconds of history." He combines and condenses the concretes by means of a wide abstraction. So even though faces cannot literally stare at history, the expression is appropriate. He makes it original because he combines miles of faces staring in one direction, which gives you a visual concrete, with the fact that it lasted only thirty seconds. He is referring to the blastoff itself, but says that the thirty seconds represent history. This dramatically condenses several complex thoughts into one image.

Since nobody can include literally every detail, what you choose to include becomes very significant. I discuss this issue in "Art and Sense of Life."[15] I begin the article with a description of a painting of a beautiful woman who has a cold sore, and use it to make the point that everything in a work of art is significant by reason of its inclusion. The same principle applies to nonfiction writing. You cannot be a verbal photographer who includes everything. Therefore, the total effect is achieved by the kind of concretes you do include, even in a journalistic account. Wainwright and I are both describing the same scene. But I select only relevant details—and in the case of the crowd, only details relevant to one overall image: its purposefulness, and the difficulties people were willing to endure. Take, for instance, the half-naked man in the hammock. It is an uncomfortable position, and reveals his ingenuity and determination.

[15]The Romantic Manifesto.

Wainwright's worst selection was "bands of the young in trunks and bikinis ran everywhere." I saw no one in trunks or bikinis, or running around. What Wainwright probably did was combine (through sheer inattention) sights from the night before the launch with what he saw right after it. There was an unbearable traffic jam along the road after the launch, and you did see a lot of trunks and bikinis. It would be appropriate to mention them if you were describing the terrible heat during the day, after the launch. But what you saw the night before was immobility. There was no place to run around, since everything was tightly packed. Even if there were a boy in trunks and a girl in a bikini running for a sandwich or to visit a friend in another car, you should not include this, because it would be a purely accidental, atypical element. Wainwright's choice of such nonessentials suggests falsely a circus atmosphere. If you are describing a huge crowd that came from everywhere, attracted by a great event, you do not introduce bikinis. If you mention them at all, it should be in some unflattering contrast to what is important. But he picks that as an essential part of the atmosphere.

Everything I select adds up to a total and is purposeful. My mind does not wander to some boy's trunks or girl's bikini. But he has no hierarchy of values, and thus no conscious purposefulness. I know what is accidental and what is typical of the crowd. For instance, take the man in the hammock. He might have been the only one, but this was typical of the kind of adjustments to discomfort that people were making. Therefore, I included him as an individual. If I had seen many girls running in bikinis for some reason, whether contributing to the event or distracting from it, I would have included that fact. But one girl doing so is an accident. Further, Wainwright does not project the mood of the crowd; if anything, he detracts from it. He uses words like "people lolled" and "they ran everywhere," so you do not know whether it is a picnic, as he calls it, or something else. His description adds up to nothing.

There are situations in which you want to describe a purposeless crowd. In those cases you do what he did: select random, contradictory bits. But he was trying to describe a purposeful event—a crowd gathered for a specific purpose. The mood of the event was visually perceptible—you could tell people took it seriously. But he does not project that.

A different approach to an event dictates a different way of writing about it. I give the view of Apollo 11 at night a whole paragraph. He makes it one subsidiary sentence. His focus is on the crowd, not on the rocket. I say as much about the people as he does, but they never steal the stage. In my article, the crowd serves to feature the importance of the event. That is how my mind organized the material. This is how basic premises direct your choice of content—of what aspect of the event you present in what manner—and you cannot calculate that consciously.

If you want subtler streaks of style which create a certain impression, observe the following: "There were tents perched at the edge of the water; there were men and children sleeping on the roofs of station wagons, in the twisted positions of exhaustion; I saw a half-naked man asleep in a hammock strung between a car and a tree." This is a choppy description. "There were" is not very elegant—it is too direct and easy. But I use it to give the reader the feeling (since Frank and I were driving past) of a montage. Again, I appeal to actual visual perception. I did not see a flowing progression, but snatches of typical sights. Therefore, I wanted choppiness in my description. What holds it together is the fact that the concretes are all part of the same scene; they add up to an impression of the size, discomfort, and exhaustion of the crowd. Later, when I say, "the same, patient cheerful flood," it would have been a bad editorial estimate had I not already given you the concretes. Had I presented a smooth, flowing sentence, that too would have been an editorial summation, whereas I wanted to show what I saw. Always try in such cases to reconstruct for the reader, by means of essentials, what you perceived.

Now consider this line of Wainwright's: "this vast picnic crowd had gathered to see the booster belch out its tremendous power and hurl likenesses of themselves at the Moon." It is disgusting. First, notice the choice of words, and keep in mind my discussion of connotation. I would use a word like "belch" only if I wanted to degrade something. While that was not his intention, it is a very inappropriate word here. And "likenesses of themselves" provides a disgusting glimpse of his ideas about human motivation.

Observe also the mixture of time elements. He is describing the night before the launch. The next paragraph begins: "By morning there were many more." So the preceding sentence about the belching and hurling is, in his mind, part of the night before. That is undercutting. He projects what he saw later and makes it part of the description of the night before, and then returns to the next morning. Therefore, his readers do not know where they are. He is trying to tell you how he imagined, that night, what the crowd was going to see. Not only is this confusing, but nothing could be more anticlimactic and more presumptuous than projecting a great event that is going to happen. He had no business doing it. This approach would be bad enough if it described a small event, because it produces an anticlimax. But considering the grand nature of this event, his presumption is dreadful.

If there is an unprecedented sight of such importance that a million people come from far away and endure terrible discomfort to see it, and the reporter says, "I know what will happen, there will be fire belching and likenesses hurled," that is presumptuous. He sees no difference between a description of the event and his own imaginary bromides about it. I would not dare do this. Every literary and philosophical premise in me would stop me. If I think the event is big, I let it speak for itself.

Had I been disappointed—which I was not, it was greater than anything I could have imagined—I would say, "I expected a big burst of fire and it fizzled." One could properly write that about some event that, for example, was oversold by press agents.

Do not project in images what you *think* an event is going to be like. Always stay behind the event. If you have any values to project (which I did), do it by means of the concretes you select, never by means of your own imaginary constructs.

Here are some more problems with Wainwright's choice of words. He said, "People lolled in the grass." Nobody lolled that night. But even if he saw, for instance, somebody sitting in the grass, the verb "lolled" destroys the description. Nobody would loll on a lawn if he had to stay awake all night in dreadful heat. If you saw those people, you would never think of a lightweight verb pertaining to relaxation. Similarly, he should not have used "picnic" as he did. Again, watch the connotations of the words you use.

His worst mistake with respect to word choice comes in his description of Apollo 11 at night: "Clearly visible through the night about 10 miles away was the Apollo 11, bathed in searchlights, a tiny stalk of light in the darkness." More than anything else, this made me furious. I had gone through the process of working to convey that tremendous visual sight. Then to see somebody with the same problem dismiss it in this way—it was most telling. "Bathed in searchlights" is a bromide. You could say "dripping with light" or "wet with light" (as I once said in *The Fountainhead*); that says something. But "bathed in light" is a bad choice of words; even if somehow you had to use that bromide, it more appropriately describes something indoors (e.g., "a drawing room bathed in light"). But Wainwright uses an inexact bromide about a sight that had enormous grandeur, instead of struggling to describe accurately those huge lights coming out of the two small figures. I almost felt like a proletarian angry at the idea of a bourgeois who does not earn his income. Wainwright did not work at it—he was inadequate to the task.

Moreover, they were not *search*lights, because searchlights move. They were huge batteries of light installed around Apollo 11 and its service tower. This is a good example of the difference between showing and telling. He uses an inappropriate conceptual summation—"searchlights"—instead of giving you the actual sight and letting you conclude that they were searchlights or some other kind of lights. He sums up, rather than showing you what he saw.

Earlier I said that you can improve your ability to write by identifying a bad passage and why it is bad; you thereby learn the abstract principles involved. I hope this comparison clarifies what I meant by that advice.

9

Book Reviews and Introductions

Reviewing books is a valid profession, if practiced properly. Its purpose is twofold: to report on and to evaluate what is published. A reviewer functions as a reporter and scout, since nobody can read everything that is published.

There used to be reviewers who had personal followings, because they were reliable. They had definite viewpoints, and you knew by what standards they praised or panned a book. I observed through the years that as these people lowered their standards and recommended bad books, they lost their followings. Today, no reviewer has a following, because none has any standards. Some openly admit the fact that they follow their feelings, while most evade it. But even the worst irrationalist will not be guided by somebody else's feelings forever. Therefore, reviewers have no function today, even among people who agree with them. If anyone reads them, it is for the reason I do: to discover what the book is about, ignoring the reviewer's estimate. That is the best reviewers can do today, and it is a disgrace to the profession.

In *The Objectivist*, we do not review bad books, because there are enough bad ideas floating around, and it would not be worthwhile to my readers to be told how many bad books are published. Not only would it have no value, but we could not keep up with them.

The special purpose of our book reviews is to help those who agree with Objectivism acquire relevant knowledge. A philosophy provides the basic principles that apply to all of existence, but it does not tell you everything. There are many discoveries and arguments, particularly in the social sciences, which are relevant to philosophy and necessary to know. For example, it is not enough to be for free enterprise on moral grounds. You must also know the historical case for it, and be able to answer the questions being raised about it today.

A corollary purpose is to help worthwhile books against the blockade of liberals on the left and religionists on the right. Little of value is published today. But those books of value that *are* published may never be heard of, given the present state of reviewing. I dread to think of how many good books have been published but went unknown. Of course, personally, that is *my* battle. So a secondary purpose of book reviewing in *The Objectivist* is to let an interested audience know that these worthwhile books exist. Few books are fully on our side; but any book whose virtues, ideologically, outweigh its errors is worth supporting. This does not mean we have to praise every book we review. It means we do not review the books we cannot praise. Since we are not a general information magazine, but one with a certain viewpoint, we are not obligated to review everything that appears.

A magazine with a general cultural viewpoint, however, *is* so obligated, though such magazines seldom fulfill that obligation. A general reviewer of books should review the whole field of books, and only differentiate between books of greater and lesser importance (by the length of the reviews and, in general, by the attention given the books). This is a legitimate undertaking, though magazines today never do it. But that is their problem and their immorality.

A magazine that undertakes to review the whole field of books requires negative book reviewing. The responsibility for assigning books is the editor's, not the reviewer's. For example, the policy of *The New York Times* is to give left-wing books to sympathetic left-wing reviewers, and right-wing books to left-wing reviewers as well.

That is dishonest and nonobjective. But suppose a magazine's policy were fair, and you received a book to review, which you found was bad. It is appropriate to write a negative review.

There are three basic requirements for a book review: (1) to indicate the nature of the book; (2) to tell the reader what its value is; and (3) to tell him briefly what its flaws are, if any. (I am speaking now of nonfiction books; I will cover reviews of fiction later.)

Point 1: The nature of the book. Do not give a full synopsis. Do not report every salient point or the exact progression of a book. This is a mistake beginning reviewers often commit. Indicate the nature of the book, but do not recapitulate it. There is an old joke where one intellectual asks another: "Have you read any good book reviews lately?" That used to be the literati's custom, and you should avoid it.

Always indicate the author's general theme. You need not describe all of his reasoning or material; merely indicate the overall direction by saying the author claims A, B, and C, and such is the theme of the book. Whether you agree with him or not is a *separate* issue (which comes under points 2 and 3).

As a reviewer, you must be skillful enough to isolate the book's essentials, and present only those. State the subject and give some idea of the author's development of that subject—the highlights and key points. (And even here you need not include everything.) But never include nonessentials while omitting key points, because that constitutes a misrepresentation. This can happen when you are in a hurry: if your space is limited, and you have not prepared a good outline, you might start listing the first points that come to your mind, although they are nonessential. But to be fair, you must include what is essential to the author's theme.

Always include some quotations that are typical of the author. This is important on two counts: (1) it gives the reader, firsthand, an idea of the author's approach, and (2) it gives an idea of his style (which is important, even in nonfiction). In a certain sense, a reader has to take you on faith. You are the middleman, and the more quotations you provide, the better you are as a reporter, because it is by means of these that the reader can judge you as well as the book. He can see whether what you allege about the book is actually supported by the quotations. I frequently read reviews in which the quotations do not fit the reviewer's evaluation (and often they are much more interesting than what the reviewer tells you). Therefore, whenever you use quotations—and use them appropriately—you provide objective evidence of your own reliability.

The difficulty is finding *brief* quotations, because a review made up predominantly of quotations ceases to be a review. It becomes a sampling, like a movie trailer, and does not tell the reader what the book is about; he does not know what there is between those quotations. So preserve a balance.

Obviously, your selection of quotations must not be distorted. If you read today's reviews, you will notice that anything can be supported by ellipses and the out-of-context quotation, which is immoral. If you cannot support a particular contention of yours by means of quotes, do so without them. It can be difficult, especially in nonfiction books, to find a quotation which is brief, yet distinctive enough to indicate the author's viewpoint and the quality of his writing.

In all writing, the principle of selectivity operates by implication. The reader will necessarily think, to the extent he trusts you, that if you select a quotation, it is representative and fair. Your selection carries weight by the fact of being selected, so be sure it lives up to your purpose—namely, to indicate the essentials of the author's approach and style. There is no profession immune from the rules of objectivity. If you are not objective in reviewing books, you will lose your following. And every writer should want a following, in the sense of having his readers satisfied rationally and having them trust him.

Suppose you review a book that has many different aspects. If the author is particularly interested in one aspect, but you focus on another which you find more interesting, that is not improper, provided you indicate both the author's interest and your own. You need not share the author's main interest in order to write a fair review.

Suppose somebody were reviewing *Atlas Shrugged* (to take an example from fiction). If he consulted me, I would say the most important aspects to cover are: esthetically, the presentation of man the hero; and philosophically, the book's ethics and epistemology. But suppose the reviewer, who agrees with the novel's philosophy, is particularly interested in its political aspects, which he stresses. That would not please me, but I would not consider it dishonest, so long as he indicates that my theme is wider than politics. His approach would be all right, because that aspect *is* in the book, only it is not as important to me as it is to this reviewer. Such a review is fair, because you cannot expect a reviewer to agree with you on every aspect of your book and to have the same hierarchy of values.

It would be inappropriate, however, if one had a totally different motive. Suppose you are reviewing a book on esthetics, in which the author presents a new theory of art. But you are primarily interested in capitalism, and thus in the single section of the book that discusses the plight of the artist in society. You then take the book as a springboard for presenting something quite different from its actual subject and theme. That would be misleading.

Fairness is always possible. The secret is to identify the facts, and then explicitly identify to yourself and to your readers what you are doing. In that way, you can be perfectly fair to an author, even when you disagree with major aspects of his book.

Point 2: The value of the book. I can state this point briefly. Indicate what is good or informative about the book, i.e., what the reader will learn from it. Here you can follow a simple rule: if you think the book is valuable, ask yourself what *you* learned from it. Select what is most important, and indicate that to the reader.

Point 3: The flaws of the book. Briefly indicate the book's philosophical and stylistic flaws. This is especially important in regard to nonfiction books of mixed premises, which are the best an Objectivist can recommend today. There will always be books of mixed premises which are valuable, but their mistakes must be indicated.

If you do not indicate the book's flaws, you bewilder your reader. It is unfair not to tell the reader the aspects of the book with which you disagree. But do not argue with the author. For example, some inexperienced Objectivist writers believe you should use a book review to spread Objectivism. But the same considerations [discussed in chapter 4] apply here, only more so. When you report on a book, you are not selling your philosophy. You are merely selling the particular values which the reader can find in this book. It is not your job to save the soul of the author. And more importantly, you must not use *his* book to present *your* ideas. That is what too many of today's reviewers do. Whether they do it to show off their intelligence or to proselytize for their own philosophy, it is a mistake.

As a reviewer, you must express your opinion. But be sure to keep your estimate separate from your report on the book. When you find flaws, it is important to indicate them and, if the issue is serious enough, to indicate what the truth is on that issue. But do not begin to argue for the correct view. Merely indicate what the truth is about some error by the author, and give a reference to where the reader can look up the proof of your point, if necessary.

In effect, your policy should be: "This book has values A, B, C, and D, which make the book worthwhile, but it has flaws Y and Z. Here is why I regard them as flaws . . ." But be sure you present the author's ideas correctly. If the author is good on certain points, do not exaggerate them and make him out to be better than he is. Likewise, if there are points which contradict your own viewpoint, do not denounce him and exaggerate his flaws. A review is not a polemic.

A polemical article has its place. One can take a book with a wrong viewpoint and write an article denouncing it and explaining why it is wrong. Even in such an article you must present the author's viewpoint fairly, so as to avoid attacking a strawman. But that is *not* a book review—it is a discussion of ideas for which the particular book you are attacking serves as the springboard.

Having examined the three basic requirements of a book review, I next want to mention two errors that reviewers often make.

The first error is to tell the author how he should have written his book. *Never* do this. You can offer criticisms without telling the author what he should have done. This error takes the form: "If the author had done so and so," or even: "The author should have done so and so." That is no longer a report or evaluation, but the attitude of a bad editor. (A good editor never tells an author how to rewrite a book; he merely indicates the flaws he finds.) It is permissible to say, for example, "The author has stated such and such, but he has not touched on these aspects." That is not the same as saying "The author should have included these aspects."

This is not merely a semantic issue. The impropriety is not only the form you use, but your intention. Telling an author what he should have done is so inappropriate that any writer should resent it. I resent it every time I encounter it, even if the book is bad, because it is presumptuous and patronizing. A reviewer's job is to report on a book and evaluate it, not to set himself up as a collaborator and to tell the author or the public how a given book should have been written. He cannot hold as the author's fault the fact that the author has a different philosophical outlook, even if it is wrong. A reviewer must inform the reader about the author's viewpoint, not substitute his own. Moreover, to say what a marvelous book you would have written is entirely inappropriate; and a reader's immediate reaction is: "Why didn't *you* write it?" Therefore, avoid telling the author what he should have done. (If you write, "The author claims it is appropriate for the government to interfere; I, however, disagree," you are not implying the author should have rewritten the line. For you are not saying the author should have accepted your views, or even known of them.)

This leads me to the second error: the failure to keep a strict line between what the author says and what the reviewer says. This problem enters into every review, because you should not entirely isolate the description from the evaluation; you must make parenthetical value judgments as you proceed. The best way to avoid the error is by explicit statement. You say, in effect, "This is the author's viewpoint; and now this is me, the reviewer, talking."

When you are synopsizing the author, you need not constantly remind the reader that you are doing so. But at occasional intervals, when you want to stress that this is something you have gathered from the book, write: "as the author states" or the like. And after every aside in which you have expressed an opinion, indicate your return to the presentation of the author's views.

In a negative review, you have to tell the reader why the book is bad and what kinds of errors the author commits (e.g., he suppresses or distorts facts, or he draws the wrong conclusions from them). But there too, be sure to keep your views separate from the narrative material. First, present the essentials of the book, and of the author's viewpoint, as clearly and fairly as possible. Then say, for example, "I think this is a bad book because the author distorts the evidence on such and such facts," and cite the proof of his misrepresentations. Then say, "From these facts he draws the following conclusion, and here is what is wrong with it." But at no time should your motive be to show the stupid author how much cleverer you are than he (which is not much of an achievement if the book is that bad). A review is not a contest between you and the author.

Your own philosophy should not be your primary focus. For instance, you write: "The author distorts facts A, B, and C, and he draws the collectivist conclusion X, which is wrong. Free enterprise did not lead to the evils he asserts; the cause was Y." Here, your own pro-capitalist viewpoint is implied. You can even, when appropriate, state it openly. But always remember that it is not your purpose to use a book to propagandize for capitalism or whatever your views might be. If the assignment is to report on a given book, that is what you should do. If the magazine did not hire you to write a hymn to capitalism, do not write one. (If that was what the editors wanted, they would have asked you for an article, not a review.)

Never use a bad book for some improper or irrelevant purpose, just because *your* purpose is "good." The end does *not* justify the means. This is what left-wing reviewers try to do. They may even know they are being dishonest and slanting their reviews, but they argue: "The author is for capitalism, therefore he is evil; I am doing this for collectivism, therefore I am good and my distortions are justified." That is the psychology of leftist reviewers, and you must not accept any part of it.

Unfortunately, the opportunity to review good fiction will rarely come up. I wish there were more fiction books to plug, but there are not. There may be in the future, however, so you should know how to handle such a happy contingency.

The three main elements to cover in nonfiction reviewing—the

nature of the book, its value, and its flaws—apply also to fiction reviewing, but with certain variations.

In regard to the first point, when you review fiction, indicate the
nature and progression of the story, but not its climax or resolution.
This is not an absolute. Sometimes the climax illuminates the whole
book, so you need to discuss it. But usually it is better to build up the
suspense and then, in effect, tell the reader, "If you want to know
how it turns out, read the book." If your review is positive, it serves
as a "movie trailer" for the book. A movie trailer selects what will
arouse the viewer's interest, and presents him with a brief montage
of the film. The same principle applies to a positive review of fiction.
Indicate what the story is about and some of its progression, but do
not give away everything. Make the reader interested enough to read
the book.

In mystery reviews it is an unwritten law that a reviewer must
never give away the solution. In a certain sense, this applies to any
serious work of fiction. If you give the reader an exact summary of
the book, you destroy the suspense, particularly if it is a book with a
good plot.

Always indicate the four main elements of a novel: plot, theme,
characterization, and style.[1] But do not present them one at a time,
like a classroom analysis. Skillfully integrate all of them. For example, when you present a paragraph about interesting events that start
the plot, at the same time indicate what kind of characters enact it.
This is not always possible, but it should be your goal.

In regard to the second and third points of book reviewing, concerning evaluation, do not read fiction as if it were merely the means
to an ideological end. It will be a long time before anyone attempts
what I did in *Atlas Shrugged*, where reviewers would be semi-justified
in thinking the fiction is merely a springboard for presenting a philosophy. That is not the way *Atlas* was written, but it *is* a very philosophical book. Therefore, if a reviewer decided that this is primarily
a philosophical treatise with the fiction as an excuse, I could not
blame him much objectively—though I would hate him personally,

---

[1] For more on these four elements, see *The Art of Fiction* and "Basic Principles
of Literature."

because it is not true. While most fiction is not as philosophical, any serious work will have *some* philosophical meaning.

But if you stress that a book is wonderful ideologically, you commit a first-class offense against the author as a fiction writer. You invert the proper hierarchy of values when you review fiction exclusively or predominantly from the viewpoint of its philosophical value. That it has some valuable ideas must be treated as pure gravy. So review fiction primarily as literature.

The main requirement for a review of fiction pertains to drama and color. If you want to recommend the book, your review must be dramatic and colorful enough to communicate to the reader some of the literary quality of the book, though in smaller scale. This is a matter of careful integration. In this regard, quotations are helpful if they are succinct and representative. They can indicate the drama, color, and style of the author.

Do not praise a book if only a few lines are good. At *The Objectivist,* a reader once sent me a children's book, recommending that I review it. She quoted a couple of lines to indicate why she thought it was wonderful. It was a poem about dinosaurs, and the gist of what she quoted was that dinosaurs perished because they did not use their brains. But the book was dreadful. It concentrated mainly on which animals were eating which, and it presented a terrible jungle atmosphere, which is certainly not for six-year-olds (the book's intended audience). It actually said nothing about the importance of the brain. The mistake this reader made was taking the few lines about the dinosaur's brain as the meaning of the whole book.

Many people are so glad these days to see one sensible touch that, dropping the context, they forget the rest and decide a book is good. But you should do the opposite: you must be most severe precisely when you think a book contains something valuable. It is fine to enjoy good passages apart from the total context. Nevertheless, in judging an entire book, you must remain objective.

Similarly, with respect to the indication of flaws, do not exaggerate some touch that you dislike into the meaning of the whole. Do not condemn a book simply because some lines may be wrong.

Never overpraise or overcriticize a book. In reviewing both fiction and nonfiction, but especially fiction, you need to preserve a clear view of the total in order to pronounce judgment. You need the full context of the book to judge fairly and objectively its virtues and its flaws (if any), and whether the virtues are more significant than the flaws. Always ask yourself whether you covered all the essentials of the book, or merely took an incomplete view and thus misrepresented it.

Turning now to writing introductions to books, the main rule is to take the word "introduction" seriously. Not all books need introductions; but if you write one, you must convey information to the reader which is relevant to a book, but is not part of it. This applies to writing an introduction to somebody else's work—whether to a classic or the work of an unknown author—or to a work of your own.

When the book is your own, the one fairly absolute rule is that the introduction must contain material which is not appropriate to the book itself, but which the reader needs to know—for example, acknowledgments.

I wrote introductions to all my collections of essays.[2] Since they are collections and not written in book form, introductions were necessary. There were two things I had to provide in these introductions: technical explanations, e.g., where the articles came from, or (where applicable) who the other contributors are; and an indication of the intellectual content. I made general remarks about the essays, which served as an integration of the total—an indication to the reader of what the book is about.

Your approach must be somewhat different if you are asked to write an introduction to somebody else's book. If it is a living author, you do what you would for a book of your own, i.e., include some general remarks about the subject of the book. But here you have more freedom than you would in an introduction to your own book, because the purpose is to state what the author cannot appropriately say himself, namely, why the book is important. This is why an introduction to the work of a living author is written by someone

[2]See For the New Intellectual, The Virtue of Selfishness, Capitalism: The Unknown Ideal, The Romantic Manifesto, and The New Left: The Anti-Industrial Revolution.

better known professionally than the author. It carries the judgment and prestige of that person, who tells the reader why he should read this book by an unknown author.[3]

If you write an introduction to a classic (e.g., my introduction to Victor Hugo's *Ninety-Three*[4]), here too you must present a generalized, integrating statement about the nature and importance of the book. Only your position is reversed: instead of relying on the prestige of your name, you must be sure not to push yourself forward too much. Your job is not to do a favor to the classic—it has already succeeded on its own. It is usually advisable, but not mandatory, to include something about the history of the book which may be of interest to a modern reader. But above all, the purpose is to tie the nature and theme of the classic to contemporary culture—to tell a contemporary reader why the book is important to him.

Do not feature yourself when you write an introduction to a classic. This issue never would have occurred to me if not for the fact that modern introductions do just that. There are all kinds of miserable little pipsqueaks who write introductions to classics in a patronizing manner, without saying anything about the book. The introduction serves only as an opportunity to show off the writer's own supposed erudition. A contemptible instance of this is Edward Albee's introduction to three plays by Noël Coward.[5] (Coward was living at the time, but was already a classic.) Albee patronizingly says, in effect, that although there is some value in Coward's plays, he does not know his job as well as Albee does. Now, if Albee wrote for two centuries, he would not be able to come near the worst play of Noël Coward's. But it is Albee's approach that I want you to notice and avoid.

Of course, as in the case of book reviews, when you write an

---

[3]See, for example, Ayn Rand's introduction to Leonard Peikoff, *The Ominous Parallels.*

[4]Victor Hugo, *Ninety-Three*, translated by Lowell Bair, introduction by Ayn Rand (New York: Bantam Books, 1962). An abbreviated version of her introduction is reprinted in *The Romantic Manifesto.*

[5]Noël Coward, *Three Plays: Private Lives, Blithe Spirit, Hay Fever* (New York: Grove Press, Inc., 1965).

introduction, you have to indicate what aspects of the book you dis-agree with, if any. Otherwise there is an implicit sanction, which would be improper with respect to your own views. Mention as clearly, briefly, and politely as possible what you disagree with or consider a flaw, but do not start a polemic with the author, and do not tell him how he should have written his book—particularly if he is not around to answer you.

If you disagree with an author more than you agree, do not write the introduction. But if the disagreement is minor, or you agree with more aspects of the book than you disagree, then you mention any disagreements unobtrusively, toward the end. Do not make them the major focus of your introduction.

Remember that "the book's the thing." An introduction is sup-posed to be a service to the reader and to the book. It cannot be an end in itself. So be sure your views are always relevant to and justi-fied by the content of the book. If they are, it is appropriate to ex-press them; do not be inhibited or humble. But it is inappropriate to use an introduction as an occasion to air views which have nothing to do with the book's content.

10

Writing a Book

A detailed account of how to write a book would itself take a book. Here, I will discuss only how to apply certain principles of article-writing to a book.

The basic principles of the two are the same. The only significant difference is *scale*. A beginning writer may not know how to apply what he has learned about writing an article to a whole book. So he must step back, abstract, and discover the equivalents. What in an article is a section or sequence, in a book may be a chapter or more; what is a paragraph in an article may be a sequence or even a chapter in a book.

There are no rules about a book's length. It can range from a monograph to a work of several volumes. Nor are there rules about how to divide a book into various parts, chapters, or sequences. All of this is determined by the nature of the subject. But in general, the purpose of subdividing a book is to aid the reader in absorbing the content, and to achieve clarity of presentation. The need for divisions is based on the fact that a mind cannot absorb everything at once (i.e., the "crow epistemology"). By breaking your material into segments, you direct the order in which the reader's mind will absorb it.

The same subject can be treated in an article, a book, or a set of books. The difference will be the level of abstraction, i.e., the degree of specificity. For example, I have often presented Objectivism in five minutes,[1] but that is not the same as the presentation in *Atlas Shrugged*. I do not present a different philosophy; if one followed all the implications of my brief presentation, one would arrive at *Atlas* (though it would take years). Any subject can be communicated very abstractly or in minute detail, and the length of a work depends on the level one chooses.

In an article, it is difficult to communicate ideas very abstractly. The higher the level of abstraction at which you write, the wider the concepts you deal with. Therefore, the difficulty in presenting something briefly—which you must do in an article—is to state your abstractions in a form clear enough to differentiate your viewpoint from any other. There is always the risk of presenting floating abstractions. (This is one reason I am concerned whenever someone, particularly a non-Objectivist, synopsizes Objectivism.) For instance, if you said Objectivism is a philosophy that stands for the good, that would be worse than a floating abstraction—it is floating smoke—because every philosophy claims this. In a *certain* sense it is true of Objectivism—only it is so generalized that it could apply to anything, and therefore is worthless as an abstraction.

In regard to a book, however, the danger is the tendency to expand your presentation into an encyclopedia. I said [in chapter 2] that you must delimit your subject when you write an article, despite the temptation to digress. That danger is much greater in a book. Since a book permits more detailed statements of a subject than does an article, a beginner might get the idea that he has the space to say anything—which quickly becomes everything. This kind of expansion is particularly problematic when your theme is broad; the broader your theme, the greater the temptation to include increasingly more subdivisions. The fact that a book does permit a certain latitude—the fact that it is like a complex orchestration with a central theme, the development of which permits a great many subthemes—can make your book spread into total shapelessness.

[1]For example, see "Introducing Objectivism," in *The Ayn Rand Column*.

Therefore, as important as an outline is for an article, it is a hundred times more important for a book. No book—fiction or nonfiction—can be written properly without an outline. There are fiction writers who claim to write inspirationally, without an outline, and it shows in their books, which are plotless and shapeless. But I know of no *nonfiction* writer who claims he can write a book that way. This is an absolute: a nonfiction book cannot be written inspirationally, because it is supposed to deal with ideas. It does not even have the excuse—which is only an excuse—that someone might offer for fiction, namely, that it deals with emotions. A nonfiction book is primarily educational; it conveys information. You cannot throw ideas at the reader and hope he will untangle them. *You* must present them so that the progression is logical and clear.

When you create an outline for a book, first make a general one indicating which parts of your argument will go into each chapter, and in what order. Then, as you come to each chapter, make a more detailed outline, as detailed as you would for an article. If you make the general outline too detailed, you will be unable to hold the total in your mind. But if you do not create the more detailed chapter outlines, you will be unable to determine the specific order of points, or to achieve a clarity of presentation, for each chapter.

In writing a book, integration of the total is very important. One young writer I know made the following mistake: he thought that one integrates a given chapter to the preceding chapter only. Consequently, in spite of a good general outline, he found it difficult to decide what to include in his second chapter. He was relating chapter 2 to chapter 1 alone, as if the integration worked backwards only. He thought that if he kept in mind what he had written in chapter 1, he could determine what would proceed from it in chapter 2 (which in a sense is true). But of course, what should constantly be in a writer's mind—and what should direct him at every stage—is the book *as a whole*.

Every aspect of a work has to be integrated into the total, whether paragraphs into a chapter or chapters into a book. The book should be one unified whole when you finish. So integrate each chapter not only with the preceding one, but also with the following ones—i.e., with the total of your book, which is not yet written.

Train your subconscious to do this. It can be difficult, which is one
reason the outline is so crucial.

Just as a sentence in your mind does not exist until it is on paper,
so the unwritten chapters do not exist until they are written. Before
then, what exists is only your outline—the abstractions which tell
you what you *will* discuss. But the actual words are not yet there.
Therefore, until your final chapters are done, little in your earlier
ones has to be considered an absolute. The only absolute while you
are writing is your abstract outline. You cannot depart from it (*unless* some essential omission or addition occurs to you, in which case
you stop and redo your outline). But as you present the concrete material within each chapter, an incalculable number of options open
up to you. For example, regarding some point of second- or third-
rank importance, the question often arises: where should you discuss
it—in chapter 2, say, or in chapter 4? While the overall, logical presentation of your subject is set in advance, you may not be able to
resolve such narrow issues without the full, final context. The principle, therefore, is to view what you have written as open to correction until you finish the book. Your book must not become an
absolute in your mind, in regard to its concrete content, until your
final editing.

Often you find certain sequences so good that you *know* you will
keep them; but even this is not an absolute. If you are that pleased
with a passage, you will probably turn out to be right. But without
becoming a relativist, be a good contextualist: do not set any such
absolutes until you finish the whole book. This requires a difficult
combination of absolutism about your value judgments and, at the
same time, flexibility about your writing. Your premise should be:
"This seems right to me within my present context of knowledge,
but three-quarters of my book, say, does not yet exist, and therefore
I allow for the possibility of making changes."

Of course, the real absolute is the page proofs or galleys. A lot of
editing will be done in galleys; when you see your work in print, it
acquires an objectivity which a typewritten manuscript does not
possess. A typewritten manuscript is too open to your corrections,
and your subconscious knows it. Your mind remembers how many
times you made corrections, and how many possibilities there were.

Therefore, everything is still somewhat provisional. But when you see what you have written in cold print, set by somebody else, it acquires a more objective finality, and some new corrections or improvements might then strike you.

Regard your book as finished only after you have gone over it as one integrated whole. Keeping in mind all the complicated threads and issues involved, you can then see whether your provisional integrations were correct.

Someone once said that a writer's most important tool is scissors, by which he meant that a writer should never be afraid to cut his own work when necessary. I have never sympathized with this attitude, because I hold this premise as such an absolute that I do not think one should boast about it. Courage is not required if your purpose is to write a good article or book, and some beautiful passage does not fit into the total context. In such a case, there is no choice involved: of course, you make the cut. Acquire that kind of ruthlessness. Make your central value the total job, not any particular passage.

Here is an example from my own experience. *The Fountainhead* is a long book with a complex theme. There were numerous subthemes (which, in a nonfiction book, I call issues of second- or third-rank importance). I determined in my outline what incidents of the plot would dramatize which steps of the major theme. But on many lesser issues or subsidiary illustrations, it was difficult to decide the best place. When I started submitting the book to publishers, I had written part 1 and about a third of part 2. In this material, I had several scenes which were well-written, but repetitive. They dramatized the same issue. Nevertheless, I could not yet decide which of them fit better, and in which part of the book they belonged. I decided I would keep every uncertain scene until I saw the total, at which time I would choose which to save. I knew that the reason I could not decide at the time was that I needed the total context. When I submitted the material to Bobbs-Merrill, I gave Archie Ogden, the editor, an estimated number of words. He pointed out that part 1 then seemed too long. I explained to him my method, and said that in the final version a third of part 1 would be cut. And that is exactly what happened. I even cut an entire, very interesting, character—

Vesta Dunning—from part 1. I felt a moment's sadness and a mild regret, and then felt nothing, because cutting her was necessary: it was that character or the total novel.[2]

This is what I mean by flexibility. It is not relativism or whim-worship. There are passages you cannot integrate into an unwritten whole, and therefore you should leave them in provisionally.

Writers who believe, consciously or subconsciously, in an "ideal," Platonic archetype of a book would never use this method, and so would torture themselves needlessly. Such writers believe there is an abstract rule somewhere in infinity that indicates which sequences should remain and which should be cut; but, of course, they fail ever to discover it.

A book is a creative product, and the possibilities are incalculable. If at some point you do not know what choice to make, it simply means all the evidence is not in, and so you postpone the decision without any self-doubt. Every piece of writing involves new problems. Reason and reality are the only absolutes, and the theme and the outline are the sub-absolutes. Everything else is up to you. Many issues are optional, and it is no reflection on you if you sometimes hesitate or are uncertain.

In fact, hesitation is often a good sign in regard to the development of your subconscious writing premises. A child writing a story will not have the choices you do as an adult writing a book. He might write inspirationally and produce, for his context, a good piece of work. But he would not yet know that there are questions over which one can hesitate. So if you hesitate, it may be that your knowledge is broad and you have grasped numerous possibilities. Finally, remember that if there was no indecisiveness, there would be no pleasure in solving a problem, nor in writing anything. Therefore, take the bitter with the sweet (which is a bromide I would kill you for using in writing).

Let us turn to a related point: do not regard your chapters as separate articles. This can be tricky, because in one sense you do need to

[2]The draft material on Vesta Dunning has been published in Leonard Peikoff, ed., *The Early Ayn Rand: A Selection from Her Unpublished Fiction* (New York: New American Library, 1983).

regard them as separate entities. (In this respect, do not take my nonfiction books as patterns, because most of them are collections of articles. Even so, I did a lot of editing to eliminate repetition and bring the articles into a greater unity. However, we are not discussing anthologies, but nonfiction books written from scratch.)

Your subject and theme are not completely covered in each chapter, only in the whole book. Therefore, you must regard your chapters as steps in an overall progression. The end is the total. The comparison to steps is accurate, because it is by means of dividing your complex subject and theme and covering them in installments that you achieve a progression which is integrated into a total presentation. But the chapters must be *steps*. Each has to be an entity in its own right—not an independent essay, but a part of your book that has covered a certain distance. At the same time, each chapter must serve as a base for the chapters that follow. It is particularly in your early chapters that you have to plan a great many future ones which will carry you through the total of the book. In that way, each is a means to the next chapter *and* to the total.

The best illustration of this process (only as a metaphor) is the passage from *Atlas Shrugged* in which Dagny has quit the railroad for the first time, and is thinking about the aimlessness of her days. She says that the proper progression of a man's life resembles stations on the way to a final terminal. Man must have an overall purpose—a career—which is in turn broken up into particular purposes. A career consists of certain goals, and each one opens the way for wider goals—for wider achievements. If you are a writer, you do not write one book and then stop; you grow with every book. If you are a properly developing writer, you do not coast on what you have learned, but attempt ever harder subjects. This same principle applies to the book itself. Each chapter is a station reached—a part of your book which has achieved something. But you do not stop at one chapter. It is not an end in itself, but the means to the final terminal, i.e., the completed book.

Do not, however, regard your chapters as one long, uninterrupted lecture; do not begin each chapter by picking up from the last line of the prior one. A book is not a continuous speech. So regard each chapter as a little whole, as an end in itself—not in content, but in *form.* The breaking of a book into chapters gives the reader a chance to absorb distinct subdivisions of your total presentation. You do not merely give him the chance to rest involved in a blank page, and then continue. You regard a completed chapter as an end in itself formally; like the book as a whole, it has a beginning, a logical development, and a conclusion—and you start the next chapter, in form, as if it were a new essay. The same principle applies to the structure of a paragraph. You indicate what you are starting with, you lead the thought to a certain conclusion, and, when that conclusion is reached, you start a new paragraph. In *content*, however, remember that each chapter and paragraph must be a (completed) part of a whole—a way station, not a terminal.

Here are a few suggestions about some lesser aspects of writing books.

Do not constantly repeat yourself for fear that your readers will forget something or go out of focus. For instance, if you depart briefly from your main subject and then return to it, do not say, "As I already discussed . . ." Trust your reader to remember and to integrate what you have written. If he does not, reminders will not bring order to his mind. If he is out of focus, your writing will not put him into focus, no matter how good you are. If you write clearly, on a level of knowledge appropriate to your reader, you must count on his focus and his ability to carry the progression in his mind.

There are exceptions to this principle. If you return to a topic only after making some other point at great length, you may need to remind your reader of that topic. If it has been, say, a hundred pages since you last made some point, a reminder may be called for (though you should not *re-prove* the point). Nevertheless, in general, there is nothing wrong with a reader having to look back; it is not your job to prevent that from happening. In fact, every reader of a nonfiction book will need to do it—with the frequency depending on his level of focus and, even more, on his knowledge of the subject. For example, if you write a book on philosophy, an intelligent layman may need to check back more times than a philosophy major. Of course, you must write so that even the layman will understand it, though he might have to do more thinking, and read more slowly, than the philosophy major.

This point about not repeating yourself is particularly important in bringing out a crucial difference between writing and teaching.

The purpose of teaching is not only to communicate knowledge, but also to instill a rational psycho-epistemology in one's students. If you analyze what a good teacher is doing, and why his students get so much out of his class, you will find that he is communicating the material in a certain order, which, by implication, trains his class to absorb knowledge rationally. In that process, he must adjust his presentation, to some extent, to the level of a particular class, since some classes are brighter or more attentive than others. Even within a given class, the teacher may repeat certain things to help the slower or less focused students. So a greater latitude is possible to him. Obviously, the best teacher cannot force a student to understand if the student wants to be out of focus, and just sits there doing nothing; the consciousness of one man is never responsible for that of another. But to the degree to which one can help another, that is what good teachers do.

These classroom methods are applicable, to *some* degree, to writing a textbook, where many subdivisions and repetitions are permissible. But textbooks aside, when you write a nonfiction book, you are not a teacher (except in the metaphorical sense of presenting certain information to your readers). You are a broadcaster, and you aim at the best receiving set for the kind of frequency on which you are broadcasting. But the choice of whether to tune in, and of how good the receiving sets are, is up to the audience. Therefore, you cannot present a subject by hammering it, through repetition, into your readers. If a teacher sees the class attention wandering, he should do something to recapture it. But it is never proper for a writer to adjust his writing in anticipation of such deficiencies on the part of the reader.

Another problem that often occurs—particularly on a first book—is the trap of the first chapter. When a writer starts a book, the first chapter is more of a revelation to him than to any reader—a revelation not in content, but in regard to the power of writing. When you start a book—and particularly your first—you grow with every chapter. By the time you finish chapter 1, you have learned so much that, as a rule, the beginning of your chapter no longer satis-

fies you. You now know how to improve it—and by the time you finish redoing it, you will have learned still more.

If you are a beginner, you often feel as if you are going to spend
the rest of your life on chapter 1. If whenever you feel you can do
better, you thus start rewriting the whole chapter, you would be
caught in an infinite regress, because you always learn from the
process of writing. If you are not a hack or a one-book author, you
improve constantly, to the end of your career. Therefore, you *cannot*
stop each time you write a first chapter—or a tenth, for that matter.
Even when you feel as if you can dance with words rather than drag
them along painfully and ploddingly, you cannot keep rewriting
chapter 1. Otherwise, you will never get to chapter 2.

This temptation is understandable; it is quite proper to stop and
edit the whole chapter once or twice. But after that, go on unhesi-
tatingly to chapter 2. Accept the fact that you are growing and that
you must stop each chapter when you feel that *at present*, this is the
best you can do, i.e., knowing that you will be able to do better, but
not now. So do not limit your development to your first chapter. You
must proceed.

Let your subconscious take its course. Do not stand in its way by
attempting endless improvements. In the end, you will have plenty
of opportunity to adjust the beginning. There will be a stage by
about the middle of the book when, because you are much more in
control of the writing, you will feel that your first chapters must be
terrible. By the time you finish the book, however, you will have acquired perspective (particularly if you do not reread it constantly),
and you will discover just how good the first chapters actually are.
Editorial improvements will always be necessary, because you have
learned so much, but they will be minor.

If the first chapters had really been bad, you would have been
stopped by legitimate problems long before you finished.

11

Selecting a Title

When you select a title, ninety percent of your consideration should be appropriateness, five percent clarity (and if it is appropriate it will be clear), and if possible, the other five percent should be drama or intrigue. As always, do not aim at drama directly.

Selecting a title is difficult because it should grow out of an integration of all your material and must apply to the work's essence. It must come more or less inspirationally—through the same process by which you get colorful touches in writing; it can rarely be arrived at consciously.

If you think I am good at titles, I assure you I am not. I find it difficult to come up with good titles, which is a common complaint of writers. As a rule, but not as an absolute, I let a title grow out of my material. Sometimes I start an article with a provisional working title, and as the material develops, some written phrase strikes me and suggests a better title. At other times, as I am writing and focusing on the subject, something that condenses the essence suddenly occurs to me (which is not a phrase in the work itself).

You may find it useful to hear how I arrived at the titles of *The Fountainhead* and *Atlas Shrugged*.

First, let me tell you about the mistitling of *The Fountainhead*.

This is not the original title, and I still do not particularly like it. The original title was *Secondhand Lives*. Everyone disliked it, including my agent and all the publishers I heard from. But I wanted that title, because it named a completely new idea featured in the book, i.e., that many people, such as Peter Keating, live by the opinions of others. Then Archie Ogden, my editor at Bobbs-Merrill, said something that changed my mind instantly: "If you use that title, you are featuring Peter Keating." This horrified me. I had missed that implication entirely.

So now I had to search for a title that would feature Howard Roark. The title I chose next was *The Prime Mover*. But my publisher objected that most people, seeing the book in a store window, would think it was about movers. He was right, though I would have taken the chance, because I do not care what superficial people might think. Still, the expression "prime mover" is not well known enough to convey the grandeur it would to someone acquainted with philosophy. Only a dedicated Aristotelian could appreciate it.

I next chose *Mainspring*, but discovered it had already been used. So I took a thesaurus and started looking for words. Finally I found "fountainhead." What I dislike about it is that the metaphor is a bit too poetic for the nature of the book. *Mainspring* would have been better, because it suggests engineering.

The most brilliant inspiration for a title of mine is Frank's suggestion of *Atlas Shrugged*, which is almost a mystery to me. I do not know how he made that integration, but it is brilliant, because it names in two words the essence of the book. When I asked him how he came up with the title, he could not explain it. It was purely inspirational; titles usually occur that way.

Atlas Shrugged was not my original title for the book, and it was a big regret in my life that I could not use my original title, which was *The Strike*. As I wrote the book, however, I realized *"The Strike"* gave away too much. But the drama behind that title was this: I first conceived of the book shortly after the publication of *The Fountainhead*. This was in the heyday of the New Deal, when strikes were fashionable and they were *all* by the Left. Today, they are passé—taken for granted. If you see pickets, you take them as part of daily life. We have a completely mixed economy, so each pressure group uses means of that type to gain something. But in those days, it was a collectivist, definitely Leftist phenomenon. At the time, I thought there would be a certain drama in having a novel with that title by *me*, who after *The Fountainhead* was well known as a "reactionary." I was being slightly subjective in that I was counting on the reputation of my previous novel. The change in title is actually a monument to how long it took me to write the book. If the novel had been published within the first five years, *The Strike* might have been all right. But from the perspective of the ages, it would have been dated, and it would not be a good title even now. But the main consideration was that *The Strike* gave away too much.

I did not change the title to *Atlas Shrugged* until about four years after Frank suggested it. I loved *The Strike*, and have a strong prejudice against titles with a verb in them—in this case, "shrugged." A title is like a name, and I have always felt a title should contain only nouns, and perhaps adjectives, but not verbs. Yet the appropriateness of this title outweighed my particular dislike, because there can be no rule against using verbs. "*Atlas Shrugged*" was so right that when Frank told it to me, I felt that this was destined to be the title. I weighed the choice carefully, but each time I considered the issue, its appropriateness and enormous condensation made me conclude that there was no better title for the book. It names everything and gives away nothing.

I even tried the title on Henry Blanke, the producer of the movie *The Fountainhead*. This was around 1947. He was an intelligent man, though not a particularly profound thinker. I told him I was considering a title for my next novel. He knew nothing about it except that it would deal with industry. I asked: "My husband suggested the following title; how would you take it? What would it suggest to you?" Then I said: "*Atlas Shrugged*." He looked as if a lightbulb had appeared over his head, and he said: "Hmm." Then he shrugged his shoulders and said: "Well, there goes the world." That was an ideal reaction, and it impressed me very much.

Let me give you some general advice about selecting a title, if you keep in mind that there are no absolute rules here.

When I say a title should be appropriate, I mean, for instance, that if you are writing about a serious subject, your title should not be humorous. Even here, it may sometimes be appropriate to use a humorous title in a bitter or faintly sarcastic way. Above all, however, your title should not be misleading.

The best example of a misleading title is *How to Think Creatively*. This excellent book is a serious psychological study of the creative process. The title, however, suggests it is a home course on how to become a genius. The book actually contains nothing on how to think creatively; it merely describes some important aspects of the process of creative thinking. (If you were active mentally, you could get from it some valuable leads to help you think creatively, but it is not a technological book; it does not tell you what to do.)

A great many interesting nonfiction books could be handicapped by a title that falsely suggests something academic, statistical, or technical. On the other hand, if you write a technical book for specialists, do not call it, for example, *The Coming Spring*. So when you do battle with commercial publishers, which is not a happy experience, do not let them put an inappropriate title on your book.

There is a superstition among publishers, which the better ones reject, that a title helps or hinders a book. It does not. They think including something sexy in the title sells the book, but it does not, particularly not today. An intriguing title does not necessarily sell a book, nor does a bad title necessarily hamper it. A book ultimately succeeds by word of mouth, which is based on content. In nonfiction books, particularly those that deal with a journalistic subject which will be dated in five years, the title might be important—not so much to sell the book, but to indicate that it deals with a contemporary issue.

Of course, do not have so ponderous a title that nobody can retain it. For example, do not select the kind of title that John Nelson chose for his article "Some Current Conceptions of Freedom: The 'Freedom' of the Hippie and the Yippie."[1] He felt it was in the academic style, and since there is nothing wrong with it ideologically, as editor I did not want to force anything optional on him. But it is a regrettable title; and in fact, people simply call it "The 'Freedom'

[1] *The Objectivist*, Vol. 8 (August 1969).

of the Hippie and the Yippie." He did not have to include "Some Current Conceptions of Freedom."

Also avoid deliberately bewildering or ungrammatical titles. Years ago some journal offered a parody on such titles which captured their essence very well. It was: *Gently the Swallow*. That names the whole modern style. It is a noun and an adverb, and irresistibly you want to ask: "gently what?" The issue here is fidelity to grammar. It is not intriguing or interesting to be deliberately ungrammatical. Titles of that kind merely indicate that the author is muddying his waters.

When choosing a title, do not be so detailed and academic that you call your article "A Few Observations on the Subject of Epistemology, with Limitations . . ." etc. On the other hand, do not be confusing. For instance, if you are writing on a current bill in Congress, do not call it "Of Higher Metaphysics" or "The Higher Reaches of Man."

Generally, in selecting a title, choose one that feels right to you. This is a sense of life issue. If a title feels right, it will be consistent with your style. Sometimes someone else, e.g., an editor, suggests a title which grates on you, even though it is good. If you get that feeling, the title will surely clash with the overall style of your book, because the psycho-epistemological elements at work here are the same as those at work in your style. They depend on your subconscious, automatic values and integrations.

Let us look at some examples. There is a good book that has two different titles, *East Minus West Equals Zero* in the American edition, and *Are the Russians Ten Feet Tall?* in the British.[2] The former is an excellent title. First, it names the essential subject and theme of the book. It indicates not only what the author discusses—Western aid to the communist East—but also his viewpoint. The form is intriguing: it is original to use a mathematical equation, but not so bewildering that no one understands it. (One minor flaw is that it could be taken as saying East = West, but most people are not

---

[2]Werner Keller, *East Minus West Equals Zero: Russia's Debt to the Western World 862–1962* (New York: G. P. Putnam's Sons, 1962), published in Great Britain as *Are the Russians Ten Feet Tall?* (London: Thames and Hudson, 1961).

so mathematically minded as to immediately translate the formula into figures. They grasp that it is a metaphor.)

But *Are the Russians Ten Feet Tall?* is a bad title. It is cheap slang, and inappropriately humorous. This expression is usually used in such a form as: "What do you think you are, ten feet tall?" and is meant to deflate somebody's pretentiousness. But this is a small issue pertaining to human vanity, and thus is not appropriate for so horrible and tragic a subject as Western aid to Soviet Russia, which is certainly not a light or funny subject. (There is a touch of humor in the first title, but it is profoundly sarcastic.)

Now what if the author had titled the book *Western Aid to Soviet Economic Development?* That names the subject, but it does not indicate the *theme*. Based on the title, the book *could* be anti-communist, neutral, or even pro-communist (arguing that Western countries do not give enough aid to Russia). In fact, the title strongly suggests a boring, statistical account, with no evaluation one way or the other. While a title cannot ultimately damage a book's sales, a neutral title of this kind would be inadvisable.

As practical advice, when you are stuck, try out a title on some intelligent friends who do not know your subject. Ask them what kind of interpretation your title suggests, particularly if it is intriguing and must be interpreted. This might bring out connotations which have never occurred to you. You might find that although they do not understand your title, the interpretations they give you are interesting and not the opposite of your intention. That could be a reason for keeping it.

In conclusion, short of avoiding deliberate obscurity, there really are no rules for selecting a title. There can be as many titles as first names. If you asked me to invent an original name for a baby, I could come up with many combinations of sounds, some attractive, and some awkward and ugly. But there are no rules about how to invent a name, except to make it pronounceable (unlike some Oriental and Balkan names that contain only consonants). A similar standard applies to titles. Make your title grammatical and appropriate to your subject, but not confusing. For the rest, there are no general rules.

12

Acquiring Ideas
for Writing

There remains one point to discuss: how to condition yourself to get good ideas for writing in the middle range. It should be clear why I waited until the end to discuss this topic. Implied in much of what I have said so far are the main premises required to get ideas for articles and books.

Let me begin with what to *avoid*.

There is one great enemy of mental activity: repression. Repression, and any premise of unearned self-doubt, blocks many minds. Self-doubt may be appropriate in your psychological thinking or in your sessions with a psychologist, but not in action, particularly not when you are trying to stimulate your mind for writing. In regard to getting ideas, you must do what I recommended [in chapter 6] for actual writing, namely, trust your subconscious. Let your mind be free to wander around a subject and to judge it. Do not set artificial constraints—such as telling yourself that this morning you will produce ideas for ten articles. Instead, assume that you are able and willing to judge reality—to judge events, people, trends, and news stories—and that although you may have difficulties later in writing a given article, at the beginning you are problem-free. If you do not censor your mind with regard to getting ideas, you can acquire a fertile, creative imagination.

Not every idea you get will be right. Some might even be preposterous. But that is what your critical judgment is for. Just as you can edit your writing, so you can later decide that an idea for an article is not interesting, or too narrow, or too broad, etc. But do not then become self-critical and conclude that your subconscious is bad and does not give you good ideas. Permit yourself to range freely over what you observe and to form ideas. You will discard some of them, but you will find others worth pursuing.

On the positive side, the main point is that to write an interesting article, you must have a theme—i.e., you must have something to say. But there is no way to find something interesting to say unless it comes from a wider premise, wider than the subject you want to discuss. The principle is that you must have some premise of more abstract interest than the particular news item or event you are writing about. And that kind of premise comes from your philosophical convictions.

Since every adult has some philosophy—some conscious convictions on its issues—the question is how to use your philosophy to get ideas for writing. (Of course, if your philosophy is Objectivism, it will help you much more, since it is consistent and can be applied to any aspect of the culture.) You must have an active interest in some aspect of philosophy (not philosophy in the academic sense, but philosophy as it applies to life). Merely to say "I would like to write an article from the Objectivist viewpoint" is to say nothing. It does not yet contain any specific lead or incentive to get you started on writing.

You get ideas according to the standing orders you have established in your mind. For instance, since I am interested in the application of Objectivism to life, and since every aspect of philosophy—from esthetics to epistemology and metaphysics—interests me, almost anything I hear or read is of great interest to me. I do not want merely to discover the right ethics and stop there. If I did, I would not get many ideas for writing. The application of my philosophy to life is a constant standing order to myself, which leads me to observe how various ideas, good and bad, work on the culture. Thus, almost anything I read is material for my writing.

You need to be an intellectual detective. You must look at a certain statement you encounter and work forward and backward: ask yourself what are the implications of that statement and, more important, what are the premises behind it? I love doing that, and I would love to train you to do it. It would save me from feeling, every time I read something terrible, that I should write an article exposing it—which I cannot do, because there are just too many such occasions.

You need not be a professional philosopher. If you want to get good ideas for articles on topics that interest you, and at the same time enlarge your perspective on your own profession, be on the lookout for ideas that pertain to your profession. If you want to be, not a narrow professional, but one with a wider philosophical foundation, consider the interests of your own profession from a broader viewpoint. Your best lead will be any issue that pleases or displeases you.

For instance, take the physical sciences. How can a scientist tie his profession to philosophy? If he wants to write about abortion, for example, he may start from a scientific or medical viewpoint (e.g., by focusing on a test for abnormalities in fetuses) and then branch out into the wider, philosophical issues. With the advance of the physical sciences and the retrogression of the humanities, we are in a dreadful state. A scientist will feel nothing but disgust for the philosophical ideas of his colleagues and the general state of the culture. He should ask himself what makes him disgusted and indignant and why. If he observes a trend he thinks threatens his profession, he should ask himself why he thinks so, and what are its consequences. He would thereby get several ideas for articles every time he reads a newspaper.

This is even truer in the humanities. A rational person in the humanities need not go outside his own profession to feel frustrated indignation. This is a gold mine for articles if, instead of merely suffering or repressing what you feel, you identify your reaction conceptually. If you are disgusted with your profession, do not simply note that it is in a terrible state. Ask: "What is irrational about my colleagues? What about their ideas makes me indignant?" You will find more to write about (unfortunately) than you will ever be able to use. ("Unfortunately," because the culture is so rich in negatives.) I am not advocating a "John Birch Society" approach, where you start by defining what you are against. But if you want to write in the middle range, you will unfortunately find it easier to start with negative articles. Since such is the state of the culture, that is what a person must do if he wants to lead a philosophical life and apply his philosophy to what he sees around him.

Of course, if you find something good in the culture, and above all in your profession, *that* should be acknowledged. That will make for a much better theme, because there are so few occasions for it today. Whether it is someone's new idea or a resolution passed or a policy adopted, if you approve of it, then instead of merely sensing that it is on the right track, identify why you find it good and what implications it has for your profession and for society. Right there, you will get more ideas for articles than you can handle at any one time (not because there are so many good occasions, but because there is so much that can be identified on such issues).

I am not saying everyone *must* use his profession as a springboard. But if you want to write and do not know where to begin, the most fertile field is your profession. That is your central concern, and any issue corollary to it will interest you much more than if you arbitrarily decide to write about, say, deep-sea diving, which does not interest you. But obviously you have more than professional interests, so if some other issue attracts you—because it is important, and you can demonstrate *why*—that too is a good source of ideas.

Incidentally, the desire for an ever-deeper understanding of your profession is a standing order you must carry throughout life anyway. At no point should you say, "I understand my profession, I am successful, so I no longer have to think about it." That attitude would be your downfall. We cannot stand still in life. We either move forward or we deteriorate. Therefore, always seek to enlarge your understanding. If you want to be creative in your profession, and not merely a hack—if you want to be young regardless of your age, so that you will be a real "personality," and not merely a mildly competent practitioner—then you need the same premise that is necessary to get ideas for writing.

Never think you know enough. I do not mean that you must doubt the knowledge you have, but that you need to enlarge it. Nobody is in the position today—and I do not know in what society one would be—of being completely satisfied with everything he can do in his profession, and with the performance of everybody around him. And that does not even take into account one's personal life. There are always personal matters that need attention, correction, and progress; and even if everything is ideal in your life, the more you know, the more avenues are open to you to go on to more complex, abstract knowledge. I am not advising an eternal treadmill, where you are never allowed to tell yourself that you know enough. Rather, you should be on the premise that you do know enough and that what you know is valid, but that you want to go further. Not only will this active standing order enlarge your professional abilities and interests, it will also give you all the ideas for writing that you can possibly use.

As an example, take the profession of teaching. If you are a competent teacher, you can tell how successfully your students learn. Some learn well, some are bright but slow, and some seem hopeless. Where would that knowledge lead you? If you want to be a good teacher, you would ask yourself: What do I know about young people's methods of learning? How do I explain the fact that some are fast and others are not? What incentive do the good students have? Have I provided such incentives, or do they bring it to class themselves? Why are the others so bad? Can I stimulate them? Up to what point is it my responsibility? At what point is it theirs? Also, I see in my colleagues' classes that some teachers are good and others are not. Why do I think so? What mistakes do the bad teachers make? What good premises do the others have?

You could not *fully* answer all of these questions in a lifetime, yet they are all important. Like all teachers, you know that you do answer these questions, though not explicitly. You make certain observations and decisions, and after a while you discover, for instance, that you can tell by his first words what a student will do or say. But if you were asked how you learned it, you would not know. You would say you can simply tell, which means you have acquired many valuable automatized premises, but never paused on the wider meaning of what you were discovering and applying. That is, you are conscious of the fact that you are improving, but not *self*-conscious— i.e., you do not monitor yourself.

Make yourself self-conscious in regard to your own progress. You will be surprised how much you will discover and how much you will stimulate your mind. For example, if you do not properly monitor some observations you make about certain students, you may decide, "When I see students yawning, I must be boring them, so I should cut this subject short." That does not lead you far, though perhaps next time you will know, by "instinct," how to present the subject more clearly or in a more interesting way. Unfortunately, for most people this is the extent of their development.

The better approach would be to identify the problem and then ask the wider questions: "If I made a mistake and went on too long, why? I thought my class was slow, you might answer, and I did not know what was enough for them, so I overexplained. How can I devise a method of better judging their level of intelligence? Also, I notice that sometimes they are interested and sometimes they are not. Are *they* on the right premise? What is their motivation? Can I discover, from what interests them, something about the basic philosophy of the majority of my students?"

Every one of these questions requires thinking, though probably not very difficult thinking, because as a teacher you have more observations than you have consciously identified. If you constantly ask yourself wider questions—if instead of asking, "How do I get through my next lesson?" you ask, "What is the principle by which I intend to get through my next lesson?"—you are putting yourself on a philosophical premise; you are deriving wider principles from concrete events. In this way, you will get ideas from every minor incident in class. Some dunce asking stupid questions might be the cause of an important pedagogical discovery. You might discover the wider principle of why he functions as he does: perhaps he was showing off or is a neurotic or is simply stupid and does not belong in your class. Whatever it is, you are learning something from the least inspiring incident. Similarly, if something good happens in class, do not think: "For once I got a marvelous student, but too bad it is only for this semester." Instead try to identify why you like the student's intellectual performance, whether there is some way to communicate it to other students, etc. Not only will you function better, but each question is itself enough for an interesting article.

This is how one applies wider abstractions to one's own life and, therefore, to middle-range articles and books. This, in essence, is how you should condition your mind to be active and to get ideas automatically. Like everything else in the mind that seems automatic, this process must be started *consciously*. Once you condition your subconscious properly, it throws you ideas unexpectedly. It may feel as if the ideas come to you spontaneously, but to mention once again that good line from *How to Think Creatively*: accidents happen only to those who deserve them. So give yourself this standing order: "I am interested in certain subjects, and I am on the lookout for any relevant event, trend, statement, or theory—which I then want to understand and evaluate." Do this, and you will condition your mind in a truly productive way.

Let me conclude this course by telling you about an incident which made a big impression on me. It is particularly relevant to the difference between an active psycho-epistemology and a conforming one. It pertains to the whole issue of how one learns something new.

When I began my first job as a screenwriter, I had some idea of how to write a script. But I did not know the technical terminology. When I arrived at Warner Brothers to work on the movie of *The Fountainhead*, I asked for a sample script, and was given one. I was also given a secretary to provide me with any help I needed. I never had to ask her a question. I simply looked at the sample and figured out what was meant by "close-up," "dissolve," "fade-out," etc. For example, I observed that "fade-out" referred to the end of a sequence.

Now, fade-out to a few years later. I am working for Hal Wallis at Paramount.

Wallis had bought an original story, which was intelligent and had good dialogue. But, he told me, he was disappointed in the screenwriter (who had also written the story) because although the story was good, the screenplay was a mess. He asked me to take a look at it.

I did, and could not understand the screenplay. It had a close-up where the action did not necessitate one; there was a long shot when only one person was in the room; and so on. None of the technical directions matched the action of the story. I asked the screenwriter how he decided where to use a particular direction. He said he had asked for a sample script to see how it was done—*and then he followed it exactly.* If the sample opened with a close-up, he opened with a close-up. If two pages later there was a long shot, he marked a long shot two pages later, etc. Ultimately, I had to make a great many changes and rewrite some sequences, and so I received part credit.

This incident impressed me, because on my first job, I too had asked for a sample script. But *I* looked for the abstract format and knew that I had to fit that abstraction to my own story. *He* took the format of his sample literally. He was a conformist. He never asked himself *why* there were certain technical indications at specific points. He never observed that the close-ups, long-shots, and dissolves followed a certain pattern. He was a ritualist, and followed the sample dogmatically, on blind faith.

I do not think this person ever wrote anything else, although he had made a promising start.

Do not think that this writer was the first person to make this mistake. It was the same one that the Classicists made in literature. They thought that the way to make a good play was to look at Greek tragedies, for example, then reduce them to a set of rules: a good play had to have so many acts, so many characters, etc. The essential error here is concrete-bound conformity, based on the premise that *someone else* understands why a script or play is written a certain way, and therefore the writer does not have to understand. It is the reliance on other people that is responsible for this error.

The psycho-epistemological point to remember is that you must think on your own. In some situations, you may find no particular guidance, philosophical or otherwise, and yet you need to learn something new. To be innovative when you are up against a new problem, you have to approach it abstractly. That is why I stress principles. Never assume that any leads you have from others must

be followed to the letter. Never assume that the concretes are absolutes for your instruction. Concretes are merely concretes.

Of course, as I said [in chapter 4], all reality is concrete. There are
no such *things* as abstractions. But abstraction *is* the human method
of classifying, integrating, and identifying concretes. Therefore,
whenever you start on a problem, ask yourself whether you are being
concrete-bound. Take a step back intellectually. Take a look at what
abstraction is applicable. If you examine a given concrete—whether
a script, an event, a situation, a news story, or a person—always draw
the wider abstraction from the concretes of the case. That is the only
way to learn, and the only way to be independent.

My story serves as a good concrete example of a proper abstraction. Use all that you have learned in this course, not as rigid rules,
but as abstract principles to be applied by your independent thinking to your particular problems.

Follow *my* method, not the conformist writer's—and best premises to you in your future careers as writers.

APPENDIX

Selected Outlines Used by Ayn Rand in Writing Articles

Editor's Note: During the course, Ayn Rand asked the class to outline several of her articles, with the aim of improving their skill in creating outlines. She then compared the results with the outlines she had used to write the articles. Because of the informal nature of these discussions, I could not include them all in the book. Ayn Rand's outline for her article "Doesn't Life Require Compromise?" and her discussion of it are included in chapter 5. But I thought I should include the remaining outlines as an appendix.

"Altruism as Appeasement" *(in* **The Voice of Reason: Essays in Objectivist Thought)**

Subject: The psychological motives behind the intellectuals' acceptance of altruism.

Theme: The evil and destructiveness of these motives.

1. Letter from young student about the motives of college liberals. The statement of a distinguished historian. (These set the subject of article.)

2. The psychological pattern of an intelligent boy, from childhood through college, and his subconscious acceptance of altruism in exchange for "permission" to use his mind to be an intellectual.

3. The malevolent universe as the result. Examples: young scientist, elderly businessman. The psychological meaning and source of such views. Corollary symptom: the elite premise.

4. Consequences in politics. The liberal's sympathy for dictatorships. The conservative's attempt to appeal to the people through emotions, not reason. The belief of both in the practicality of dictatorships.

5. The enormously evil consequences in ethics. The belief that the more evil a person or party, the more powerful. The attempts to seek the favor of the evil and to blacken the nature of the good.

6. The influence of moral appeasers in the field of modern art.

7. The gradual erosion of a moral appeaser's sense of values. His ultimate turning into one of the boys and becoming anti-intellectual.

8. The nature and fate of the average man. The proper course for an intellectual to take.

"America's Persecuted Minority: Big Business"
(in Capitalism: The Unknown Ideal)

Subject: Antitrust.

Theme: The moral and political evil of antitrust.

1. Introduction. Convey the moral-psychological mood and meaning of dictatorship. This is the position of businessmen under antitrust laws.

2. The origin of antitrust laws. The present situation, the contradictions and nonobjectivity.

3. Brief examples, showing the trend getting worse.

4. The real meaning: the penalizing of ability.

5. Who profits by antitrust? The incompetent businessman and the power-lusting bureaucrat, whose tool is fear.
6. The General Electric case. Its result: terrorization.
7. Recommendation: Re-examine and eventually abolish antitrust. Businessmen as representatives of freedom.

"Argument from Intimidation" (in The Virtue of Selfishness)

Subject: Identification of a new logical fallacy: the argument from intimidation.

Theme: The moral evil of that argument.

1. Description and definition of argument from intimidation.
2. Psychological root of argument: reliance on moral self-doubt. Story of the Emperor's New Clothes as example of the basic pattern.
3. Examples of argument in today's public and private life.
4. Causes of argument's success: mysticism and social metaphysics.
5. Examples in college classrooms and in politics.
6. Weapon against argument: moral certainty. Proper and improper use of moral judgment in intellectual issues.
7. Proper attitude: Patrick Henry quote.

"Bootleg Romanticism" (in The Romantic Manifesto; *outline refers to the original version of the article in* The Objectivist Newsletter *[January 1965])*

Subject: Humorous detective stories.

Theme: The moral evil of apologetic romanticism.

1. The relationship of art to a culture, generally.
2. The composite picture of man that emerges from today's art. The psycho-epistemological motives of such art leading to the cult of depravity.

3. A still lower step, morally, is found in cheap thrillers. Description of thrillers as primitive form and remnants of romanticism.

4. The meaning of humor. The two types of moral cowardice.

5. The humorous thrillers are laughing at values and at man the hero. They are apologizing to the gutter school of literature.

6. The popularity of Spillane and Fleming as examples of people's need of romanticism and of heroes.

7. The gulf between the people and the intellectual elite. Example: *The Avengers*.

8. Analysis of *The Man from U.N.C.L.E.*

9. The motive and the performance of the producers of the James Bond movies. The immorality of the Maibaum interview.

10. The irrelevance of the naturalistic arguments of the thriller's enemies.

11. The real psychological meaning of thrillers and their heroes. Comparison to naturalism. Example: *Marty*.

12. The moral guilt of producers and public in treating romanticism as bootleg merchandise.

"The 'Inexplicable Personal Alchemy' "
(in Return of the Primitive: The Anti-Industrial Revolution)

Subject: Kamm's news story about young Russian rebels.

Theme: The psychology of the Russian rebels as contrasted with the young rebels in America.

1. Reasons why the news story impressed me (literarily and personally).

2. The nature of the "personal alchemy." The conviction that ideas matter. The inability to believe in the power of evil.

3. The young rebels' nonconformity and probable socialistic "idealism." (The reason why a dictatorship has to keep destroying the best among its subjects.)

4. The young rebels' good will as the cause of their arguing with Secret Police. Example: the statements of three of the rebels on trial.

5. The meaning of "abroad" to a young Russian idealist. A symbol of justice.

6. As contrast, what is "abroad" today? The nature and psychology of today's American young rebels. The young Russians are fighting for the freedom of the mind. The young Americans are rebelling against the tyranny of the mind.

7. The cultural destruction of the American idealists. Both East and West are dedicated culturally and educationally to the destruction of the mind.

8. Practical recommendation: The only way to help Russian rebels is by ostracism of the Soviet government and all of its sympathizers.

"The Psycho-epistemology of Art"
(in The Romantic Manifesto)

Subject: Art.

Theme: Definition of the nature, purpose, and source of art.

1. Introduction: The cognitive position of art. Its surrender to mysticism.

2. Art answers a need of man's consciousness. To understand this, we have to know the nature of concepts, and then the nature of cognitive and normative abstractions.

3. Metaphysical value judgments. The need of metaphysical base—and its difficulty psycho-epistemologically. *This* is the field of art.

4. Definition of art. The psycho-epistemological function of art. (Illustration: art and religion.)

5. Example of the process: Babbitt.

6. Art and ethics: The need to concretize normative abstractions. Example: Roark.

7. Mention of didactic values and literal transcriptions in art. Romanticism and naturalism.
8. Existential consequences of art. Examples: Greece and the Middle Ages.
9. Introduction of need of further discussion, such as sense of life.

INDEX